Learning to See = Seeing to Learn

Vision, Learning & Behavior in Children

Dr. Patrick T. Quaid

Learning to See = Seeing to Learn: Vision, Learning, and Behavior in Children
By Patrick T. Quaid, Optometrist, Ph.D.

Published By:
Zuhrick Publishing - a division of Zuhrick Inc.
Toronto, Ontario, Canada
www.zuhrick.com

ISBN: 978-1-9990592-0-0

Cover Design by Artists Tree
Cover Photo – ccaetano/bigstock.com
Back Cover Photo of Dr. Quaid - Corey Persic and Katie Yamamoto of Kinetic Labs
Photograph of Dr. Susan Barry by Rosalie Winard.

This book provides general information. Always consult your health professionals for advice on what is best for you.

Printed in the United States of America
First Edition

ACKNOWLEDGEMENTS

I consider myself blessed to be involved with COVD (College of Optometrists in Vision Development, www.covd.org), a truly wonderful organization whose mission is to spread the word on Optometric Vision Therapy & Rehabilitation (OVT) and to enhance lives.

Two colleagues who have been a massive influence on me are Dr. W.C. Maples and Dr. Dan Cunningham. I truly believe that people who "walk into your life" do so for a reason.

My Ph.D. supervisors, Professors John Flanagan and Trefford Simpson at the University of Waterloo, in addition to Dr. W.C. Maples and Dr. Cunningham, have quite simply opened up doors I never thought possible.

My academic years gave me the research knowledge, but "WC" and Dan opened my eyes to what real Optometric Vision Therapy & Rehabilitation ought to be. I owe these people a debt of gratitude for showing me the right path to treating patients properly and giving them a chance at dignity and the ability to thrive, and not just survive, in life.

I would also like to thank Dr. Eric Singman MD PhD, Head of Neuro-Ophthalmology at Johns Hopkins for his wonderful and insightful conversations on visually related topics over the years. We have written a book chapter together recently in a medical textbook, *Neurosensory Disorders in Mild Traumatic Brain Injury*. This book was mainly directed at doctors on the effects of concussion on the visual system. A topic for a whole other book by itself - now there is a thought! Eric, you are a true friend and scholar and have inspired me think at every turn. Thank you for your friendship and wonderful attitude to learning!

Dr. Larry Komer, MD is a colleague, author, and friend. He is one of the trusted circle of experts I consult. Dr. Komer is one of those people with curiosity and imagination who also brings a caring heart to his functional medicine practice. I was pleased to contribute a chapter to his important book, *New Hope for Concussions, TBI & PTSD* that was co-authored with his wife, Joan.

Thank you also to Dr. Glen Steel (a.k.a. "Bubba") for your contribution to the book, it is very much appreciated.

We are grateful for the chapter written by Dr. Susan Barry. Dr. Barry is the author of an insightful book, *Fixing My Gaze: A Scientist's Journey Into Seeing in Three Dimensions*. Her leadership in our field and her valiant story continues to inspire us all.

Jenny Fountain and Karen Fairley shared wonderful insights in the book from an educational perspective. These chapters give parents and healthcare professionals a guide through the IEP process and a window into the important role of teachers in the early years.

Thank you to each of the talented and thoughtful contributors who shared their expertise and their passion through the chapter they wrote.

A book is enhanced by the flair that a graphic designer brings to the publication. A special thank you goes out to Patricia Meuser-Kristy of the Graphic Gourmet for her fine work. www.graphicgourmet.ca

Our videographers support the book and make some of the big ideas accessible in a different media. We recommend Corey Persic and Katie Yamamoto of Kinetic Labs for your projects. Rosalie Winard photographed Dr. Susan Barry.

Thank you to Dr. Don MacQueen, who helped me with my first clinic in terms of building it (and ran my "first buck" through the POS machine.) Thank you for always being a friend Don.

Stephanie Beaudette has from the bare-bones start tirelessly and bravely followed me into the world of vision therapy. You faithfully ran the clinics. Thank you for your trust and support Stephanie. It has been invaluable, and I thank you for the steadfast trust you have always had in me. Kevin Beaudette, you have a breath-taking work ethic. You have been instrumental in building our two new clinics, and you are a relentless pursuer of perfection and accuracy. I thank both you both from the bottom of my heart for helping me to make the clinics a reality. I am proud to call you friends.

Let me add a massive thank you to all of the doctors, therapists, managers, and admin staff within our clinic group and all vision therapy clinics worldwide. You are the folks making the magic happen here - on behalf of parents and children everywhere that you help on a daily basis - thank you.... thank you!

Let me express my appreciation to the Government of Ontario in Canada for having the foresight to help fund some of these re-search projects within our clinic over the years. It began during my post-doctorate and continues to support our research, in the form of SR&ED grants.

I would also like to share a special thank you to Grant D. Fairley. He coached and guided me through the book writing process. Most of my writing is for research journals. Grant has been very courteous in guiding me into writing in a way that is more accessible to a larger audience and especially the *parents*.

To the entire Irish Quaid clan, you listened to my thoughts on this book many times. Thanks for always quietly supporting me in the background.

Thank you goes to Ayleen Quaid, my wonderful daughter, who is turning seven soon. Thank you for allowing me to spend time writing this book, often with you sitting quietly beside me and just watching. Sometimes sitting on my lap quietly, actually allowing me to think. You are a joy as I watch you develop and learn. When you get older and understand what I have spent that time on, hopefully, you see that it was to make other children just like you be able to learn to read the way you have. You are reading at a grade 3 level in grade 1 for a reason, and every child deserves to love learning this much. You are an "old soul," and I love you for it.

Finally, saving the best for last, thank you to my wife, Zuhal. You always believed in me and encouraged me - in good times and bad. You have truly taught me what love and dedication is.

Patrick T. Quaid, Optometrist, Ph.D.

TABLE OF CONTENTS

DEDICATION

In 2004, the year before I finally finished my Ph.D., my mother, Kay Quaid, passed away from ovarian cancer at the young age of 53. I dedicate this labor of love to her. She was diagnosed on a Monday and passed away within a week. Sadly, I did not get to say goodbye. She passed away while I was at 30,000 feet above the Atlantic Ocean.

Although she never got to see me get my Ph.D. from the University of Waterloo School of Optometry & Vision Science in Canada, which would have tickled her pink, she did get to see me become an eye doctor and get married to a wonderful woman who has supported me in every endeavor to date.

Unfortunately, I did not get the opportunity to treat my mother's visual issues. She did so much for me as a child to encourage me, despite my significant speech and vision issues.

So, here is my response, in book format, to those wonderful parents and children who are the bravest folks I have ever met – hands down.

It is often frowned upon as a healthcare professional to self-identify with your patients. Given my own personal history, when I see the immense struggles these kids go through at school, I do empathize. Of course, in my professional role, I limit sharing too much of my own personal experiences, but I certainly have learned to channel that passion into doing my utmost, to try to rehabilitate every single patient as fully as possible, using our research-based protocol as my tool. This tool, of course, is always being refined as we learn more and more about these visual-based issues that often impede the ability of a child to learn. I firmly believe, however, that my personal experience, in addition to the visual history of both my parents, is more valuable *than a hundred Ph.D.s.*

I write this book to honor them and all the parents of learning-disabled children. They are remarkable people. Parents of learning-disabled children are the most courageous group I have ever met. My colleagues and I see this every day in our practice. The effort that these parents invest in finding solutions for their children is just staggering. These dedicated parents are indeed the unsung heroes of the cases that we deal with in our clinic. Their dedication to their children is often simply astounding.

I not only dedicate this book to my mother, but to all the parents who are working tirelessly to get to the root of their children's struggles. Vision is not the only factor, of course, but I firmly believe it is a critical factor overall.

As you will learn in subsequent chapters, these visual issues are much more pervasive than you think and are often incorrectly labeled as other entities, such as "Attentional Issues" or "Learning Disabilities". ADHD as just one example, is solely a symptom-based diagnosis with the symptoms overlapping massively with untreated visual issues. It is vital that we try to remediate and diagnose our children as much as possible, to help every child reach their maximum potential. This is absolutely possible! My mother would be proud.

FOREWORD

Patrick Quaid wrote this book from his heart.

People who have had their lives changed for the better by vision therapy tend to be very passionate about the subject.

My first exposure to vision therapy was life-changing. A colleague had a child who hated to read, had severe behavioral problems, and nothing she tried made a difference. After an evaluation by a developmental / neuro optometrist, it was found that this child saw double when he tried to read. When asked by his mother why he had not told her, his response was, "You never asked!" He had looked at his classmate's paper in the classroom, and it also looked double, so he assumed everyone saw the same way. He thought that he was the only one who could not figure it out. After a program of optometric vision therapy, he read twenty-two books that summer. He wanted to read!

This experience changed my career. I focused on helping optometrists who provide vision therapy. I also wrote press releases for the College of Optometrists in Vision Development. This provided me the opportunity to interview many people who had amazing stories that they wanted to share.

When most people think of vision problems, trouble seeing the board in the classroom, or having difficulty seeing things in the distance, are what come to mind. People assume that because their child can see far away that their vision is also normal when reading. While it is true that if someone has trouble seeing in the distance, they have a vision problem, it is not true that if someone can see in the distance, their vision is functioning normally when reading. Being able to see the letters on an eye chart from a distance of twenty feet is only one of seventeen visual skills critical to reading and learning.

It can be confusing to parents (and the child) when a child can read text out loud but not remember it. The incorrect, but the typical, assumption is that if the child can read it out loud that they can easily see the words, so something else must be wrong. The key here is that it takes a tremendous amount of work for the child to actually see the letters, so they don't remember what they read. If you can imagine trying to read while you are jumping up and down, it takes so much energy just to read the text; you do not have the mental reserve to also remember what you've read. For someone who is struggling with an eye coordination problem, this is their life.

Vision therapy can change lives.

Children who struggle to read deserve the opportunity to learn to see so they can see to learn - so much of their future depends on it.

Toni Bristol

INTRODUCTION

My mother understood the impact of what vision problems can do to someone's ability to learn. She knew how profoundly that could affect a life. My mother lived with a condition called Refractive Amblyopia, commonly known as a "lazy eye." This is a term I detest. After all, if you had a poorly functioning leg, imagine if people called it a *lazy leg*! It may imply subconsciously and incorrectly that the child is lazy also.

The condition affected almost every facet of her life. She had always struggled with reading, which always bothered her, but she also never learned to drive. When my parents were growing up, in the 1950s and 1960s, it was relatively common not to finish high school. My mother never completed high school. She always fell asleep when she tried to read. Knowing what I know now from my training, I can diagnose, that her visual status stunted her abilities in many ways. It made it difficult to read and interfered with her ability to learn to drive a car. She always told me how much of a gift it was to her when I prescribed her first pair of reading glasses. Unfortunately, at that time I was still in optometry school. I did not appreciate how many other issues "beyond 20/20," were present in my own mother's visual system that still required intervention. At the time, I was still wrestling with my issues.

Healthcare professionals have a vital role at the beginning of this process. Where do parents start? It is an emotionally stressful time for us whenever our child struggles. Parents value the insights and experiences of the healthcare team to guide them. How does someone navigate the system? Where do you find a GPS for the healthcare system? How do the parents pin down the source of reading-based learning difficulties? Hearing, speech, and vision need to be thoroughly assessed in detail when dealing with children with these issues. The natural questions of the parents will be, "Where do I go?" and "What do I do?"

Screenings or routine assessments are usually just not enough; this mantra cannot be preached loudly enough. Routine assessments are fine for routine cases that are not struggling (i.e., a routine eye examination for a child with no academic concerns.) However, when issues are present, we need to do a nose dive into the visual skills, hearing skills, and speech skills of these children in a thorough way.

The skyrocketing rates of reading-based Individualized Education Programs (IEP) in our school systems tell us that there certainly are other factors at work. The high use of cell phones and other devices may signal that parents are not reading to their children as much as they used to. However, the vast majority of parents I encounter are doing everything in their power to help their child succeed. Their efforts need to be rewarded with a more detailed assessment.

It is important as healthcare professionals who help children with learning difficulties to assist the child's parents. An important point for parents to understand is that hammering tutoring and homework to improve academics may not always be the answer. It may be that their child has a visual issue. We need to be more logical about how we think about reading challenges. We need to determine first what type of reading issue the child has, and then tailor the type of remediation that will address the underlining cause. The phrase, "Diagnosis Before Prognosis" needs to be always in the forefront.

As discussed elsewhere in the book, educators have some of the most important and early contacts with the children and the parents. Equipping the early-years teachers and other professionals in the education system with this knowledge will enable them to engage and assist the parents effectively. There is such a deserved bond between parents and the teachers that much can be accomplished through that relationship. Outside of the family circle, educators tend to be a child's most committed and motivated caregivers. Educators who can make the connection between seeing to learn and learning to see will bend the opportunity curve upward for those children. What a bright future their students will have when they can apply all of their potentials because they truly see the world around them.

We should not be trying to put all children with reading issues into tutoring or phonetic awareness programs, without proper assessment and diagnosis of both their verbal/phonetic skills and their visual skills, including measures of visual memory and oculomotor skills. This idea not only makes sense clinically, but it also makes sense ethically. These children, if not remediated to their full potential, can also lose precious years by continuing to fall behind. This loss translates into a mountain of catching up after remediation. The longer it takes to diagnose the visual issue, the longer it will take to catch up. In fact, according to the National Institute of Child Health and Human Development, it takes four times as long to intervene in the 4th grade as it does in kindergarten because of brain development and because of the increase in content for students to learn as they get older.

I genuinely hope that this book will inspire professionals from multiple disciplines to have an open discussion about visual function, hearing issues, developmental history, and home environment. This will help us all better serve children who are struggling to "learn". This collection of research, experience, and ideas is our attempt to unveil vital progressive connections between vision and learning. It is to give hope and a new understanding to educators, parents, and professionals alike, trying to solve the challenges of learning disabilities. Be that reliable GPS voice that reassures parents they will find help for their child.

"You can have great eyesight but terrible vision."

PATRICK T. QUAID

DO YOU SEE WHAT I SEE?

KAREN M. "CARI" FAIRLEY

When I first heard Dr. Quaid's presentation that we "learn to see," I was intrigued. As a psychology major, with a keen interest in biology, I studied the brain and the visual connection. As a teacher, my experience has shown me the importance of vision in learning, but no one had ever expressed the idea that we must learn to see. Many think it is a natural process; I had too. If you can see the board and read the text in a book, was that not enough?

Throughout my career, I have been involved with many children who displayed learning challenges. Often, those challenges involved their comprehension and visual processing. It was as if something was missing, between what they saw and then what they understood of what they saw. Often, it was the other way around. A bright and articulate student struggled to write even the simplest of sentences or "connect the dots" from what they read in textbooks or saw on the board. Things did not connect, no matter how much effort the student put into the assignment. My experiences were typical of most teachers who work in the early years and elementary education.

Learning to see – seeing to learn. It became one of the most significant "Wow!" moments for me as a teacher. This realization was a whole different perspective on how our brain processes our vision. I now have a new understanding of many of the challenges that some of my students might have. It explains that missing piece. The rest of the book will explain these crucial concepts. Let me share with the parents reading this, how educators pay attention to the learning process with their students.

So much happens at school. As a teacher, my task is to help my students on this lifelong journey of education. Over more than 25 years of teaching, with three different school boards, the primary and junior students I have served are each part of my story. I value the privilege of being a small part of their story, too. It is especially fulfilling to share those "ah-ha!" moments when a student experiences the wonder of learning.

Do you see it? Do you understand? Do you comprehend? These are typical teacher questions. Comprehension is that complex process that takes all the student's experiences and makes sense of it.

How are you interacting with the world around you in the classroom, on the playground, and in the gym? Do you comprehend what is there? Do you understand what is happening? It is a whole person question that includes your mind, emotions, social relationships, physical health, learning skills, character traits, and so much more.

Life in the classroom is about many things. Learning is the occupation of being a student. It happens through many experiences that encourage discovery, imagination, comprehension, development, social skills, exploration, inquiry, and association. The formal subjects are many, including language, math, science, the arts, a new language, and social sciences. Learning is challenging, an adventure, and often very satisfying.

One of the most common instructions in any classroom is, "Look at the board."

Not so long ago, those were only chalkboards. Then, they became whiteboards with their erasable markers. In many classrooms, with the introduction of the variety of online and computer technologies available, teachers may now find a smartboard. A teacher or student can touch the smartboard to move, change, and interact with the material presented. Virtual reality in the classroom is already available. Someday, teachers may have a Star Trek type holodeck for their learning environment!

Whatever medium or media the board might be, if a student can not see the board, their learning potential can be severely challenged. The frustration a student feels when they struggle to see clearly will often show up in their behaviors. They may act out, distract others, and be unable to sit still. Up they get out of their chair to sharpen their pencil multiple times during an activity – anything to avoid the discomfort they feel when they can not see well. Some of the vision challenges are seeing at a distance, while others struggle to look at their books or handouts. Their problem seeing becomes problem behaviors, and before long, they can become a problem student.

With training and experience, teachers know to observe each student's character traits and learning skills that affect their education. These can include responsibility, organization, collaboration, self-regulation, cooperation, and respect. These social and learning skills are as critical as their skills needed for reading, writing, math, science, and other subjects that indicate their academic level. Oral communication and active listening skills are also vital, of course. The teacher's role is to assess each student at whatever level they currently function at, in each subject. A student might be excellent in language, struggle in math, and be typical in science. So, while each student is in a "grade," no student is exactly at grade level in every subject. Differentiated Instruction is the term that describes all the accommodations that teachers put in place daily, to help students succeed to the next achievement level of their educational journey.

A student who is struggling, however, may have a particular learning issue that can globally affect all their subjects. They will send signals that alert the teacher that all is not well. There can be moments when they have a blank stare. When asked something they should know, yet cannot answer, because they have tuned out, it becomes clear that something is holding them back.

Teachers can gain clues about a new student's strengths and weaknesses from their prior experiences in the classroom. These perspectives come from conferencing with their previous teachers and reviewing their academic and student records.

Often within the first week of a new student entering a classroom, there will be indications that a student may have issues that interfere with their learning. They may struggle to understand what seem to be clear instructions, be unable to work independently, be easily distracted or distract others, and find concentration difficult. Some of these indicators will appear in their answers and interactions with the material. Eventually, it will be evident through the behaviors. Some students show their frustration by acting out, rubbing their eyes, complaining of headaches, fatigue, daydreaming, temper tantrums, and even wanting to leave the classroom.

Kids with poor visual memory tend to read "out loud" or "whisper the text to themselves" to re-enforce the auditory component. That makes sense if the visual system is not functioning well.

My experience has been that many of the children who struggle to see are very bright and often are particularly strong in their oral communication. When they become frustrated in the learning environment, their strengths are lost to the distracted behaviors.

A teacher's first course of action is to meet with the parents. At the meeting, you discuss the student's progress and challenges. If the child seems to be working below their potential, I often will say that I am concerned and suggest that it might be helpful to take some next steps. The first steps usually include consulting their primary health-care provider, to have a child's vision and hearing checked, before moving to more educational testing.

This conversation can be awkward for parents to have. It starts them down a path with so many questions. What does this mean for my child? What did I miss? Is it a problem we can solve? What will it cost? Will my child be labeled? How long will it take? Will my child have all the opportunities I hoped and dreamed that they might have? It can be an anxious time. I try to reassure parents that these are questions and not a diagnosis. That is for others to assess. Like most health and wellness decisions, early assessment, and beginning whatever the next steps should be is an advantage. If there is something that your child needs, the sooner it is addressed, the better it will be for the student and the family.

While my profession is teaching, I also wear the hat of being a parent. My husband and I have been on the other end of those discussions with teachers for some of our children. As much as I knew from my professional training and experience, I still had all the typical feelings and worries that any parent would have. In our case, one of our children went on to have an IEP (Individualized Education Plan or SEP – a Special Education Plan in the U.K.) created. This plan was a great help for him to succeed in both elementary school and high school. We were blessed with great support from a team. Our physicians, guidance counselors, learning support teachers, school psychologist, and administrators made time for our child, as they do for all the children they serve.

When children's needs are met, the improvement is so rewarding. When those who need glasses first come to class with them on, there is a moment of wonder and amazement. I have seen students light up when they realize what they were missing. When they come into the classroom and look around, they point to so many new things that they had never noticed before. They are surprised, delighted, and excited!

In my experience, the student's behaviors settle right down. Their confidence increases, and they participate in class, as never before. Their potential to learn is unlocked. The world is now there for them to explore in a whole new way.

Throughout this book, you will learn there is so much more to vision than, "Do you need glasses?" Asking questions to ensure that each student comprehends their experiences is critical to a good education. Be grateful whenever a teacher may ask you to discuss how your child is doing. It is an opportunity for something better.

Do you see what I see? It is so satisfying when your student can finally answer, "Yes!" Now, they have the opportunity to learn to see and see to learn.

"nobody cares how much you know, until they know how much you care."

THEODORE ROOSEVELT

W. I. G. O.

What Is Going On?

That is the question for every teacher. How is your student doing?

Parents want their child to thrive in school and life. How is my child doing?

What is going on in a child's visual system?

Here are some clues.

A list of observations when a child has visual issues:

1. Taking far too long to copy information from the board to a page and vice versa.
2. Difficulty remembering how to spell and tending to spell the word how it sounds most of the time.
3. Losing their place a lot when reading, skipping lines, missing whole words or word endings, (using their finger or a ruler to track often helps them).
4. Frequent eye rubbing and/or squinting.
5. Difficulty sustaining attention close-up, particularly when reading.
6. Substitutions when reading out loud (saying something similar to what is there but not exactly what is on the page, sometimes will interfere with meaning).
7. General avoidance and dislike of reading overall.
8. Unable to write on the line and uses different sizes of print, (i.e., inconsistent), when forming letters.
9. Seeming difficulty to maintain attention overall.

10. A noticeable difference between their oral and aural skills (i.e., speaking and listening) versus their visual skills (i.e., reading and writing).

TO KILL "TO KILL A MOCKINGBIRD"

Imagine for a moment you are back in school. You sit at home in your room on a weekend morning, knowing full well that you have a reading comprehension assignment, with written questions and of course, it is due Monday. You have been dreading this task, but you have to do it. You don't have a choice. It's bad enough that you stammer when you have to read aloud at school, and kids mock you from the back row when you cannot "get those t-words out," but that is not the worst of it. The toughest time is when you have to read yourself, "in your head." Nobody hears that part.

You pick up the book, To Kill a Mockingbird, the book your English teacher said, "Everyone should love," and you dread that familiar feeling. Your eyes start to dance on the page, seemingly with a mind of their own. It does not start straight away. It never does. You know the first few paragraphs will be fine; it always worsens the more you read. What frustrates you is not understanding why your eyes cannot seem to keep their place on the page. Why do I always feel the need to re-read each section a few times to understand the book?

After three paragraphs, there it goes. The eyes start their "dance." It gets harder and harder to find the next line. Most of the time, you skip to the wrong line or even re-read the same line by accident. Even though you sometimes use your finger to keep your place, or a ruler to keep your line, your eyes slow you down. You want to read faster and with greater understanding, but no luck. How frustrating! Worse, the words now start to drift in and out of focus, and you start to get "the headache." That dull achy feeling that feels like it lives behind your eyes. You close your eyes, rub and blink them a few times, and it works, but never for long. Why is it easier for me to understand when my brother reads to me? When I read the words myself, I am a mess after a few paragraphs.

The eye doctors say you are fine and that you, "see 20/20". Your mom and dad think you have concocted this story to get out of reading. What you are thinking is, "Why is it so hard for me to read? Why can't I read like my friends? Why is it so much work for me? Maybe something else is wrong with me? Maybe I am just stupid. I hate reading!"

Your self-esteem has not only fallen off the rails, but it's left the rail yard entirely.

Our children are our most precious assets. The previous paragraphs are a brief glimpse of my life for most of my primary and early high school years. I had a stammer and an unaddressed vision issue. It was hell. Learning difficulties take many forms, but the ones not outwardly visible are the most overlooked and as a result, the most under-treated. My speech issue was treated much earlier than my vision issues. Why? This is due to the fact that students, teachers, and friends, *noticed* my speech issue. They could hear it. Little did they know I had visual problems that were much more debilitating, despite my still being able to, "see 20/20".

Of course, no parent wants his or her child to stand out. Issues such as speech impediments are hard to miss and therefore usually tackled earlier. Given that at least 40% of the brain's machinery is primarily visual in nature, and that up to at least 16 visual skills, other than "20/20" are involved in reading, it is hard to understand why vision beyond "20/20" still receives such little attention in the realm of reading and written output-based learning difficulties. This is especially evident when these two specific issues (more so reading) represent over 82% of all learning issues. The current mantra appears to be, "So long as my child can see 20/20 on the eye-chart, their eyes are fine." The sad fact is that nothing could be further from the truth.

Although my high school life was tough, I consider myself fortunate that I went through these issues. It now informs my clinical work and research approach, as our team continues to publish in peer-reviewed journals. I can tell you, first-hand, how my vision issues affected me as a child but as an eye doctor, I can now also understand it from a causative perspective, and oddly, I am very grateful for my struggles. The fact that I was able to overcome these visual issues is one thing, but it is quite another to use this gift, to now research and alleviate the same challenges for others. My current research and clinical work is immensely gratifying, not just on a professional level, but on a personal level. The research we are now publishing is helping others conquer the same demons that plagued my academics for years.

I was one of the lucky ones. I had parents that cared, a sibling that truly cared. I was also fortunate to get my speech issues addressed and my vision addressed "enough" before optometry school. This allowed me to progress, albeit with a lot of effort. I managed, however, to accelerate my "road to recovery" in essence, by self-learning and "figuring out my issues." I puzzled it out over time. What I have gone through to learn what I have, no child should have to "figure out" on their own. When we get a new piece of electronics we get a user manual, yet isn't it odd that there is no real "user manual for maximizing your child's learning potential"?

The irony is that now when I read "To Kill a Mockingbird" to my daughter, Ayleen, she loves it! Having been taught all the visual skills and tricks, she is easily reading now at a mid-grade 3 level, even though she is currently in grade 1. I am immensely grateful for the visual skills that have been taught to me over the last 15-20 years. I can now safely say, I am "killing it" when reading "To Kill a Mockingbird"! There is no reason why I would not wish to convey the gift of effortless reading and a love for learning onto every child I can. Anything less would be offensive to me frankly. To be clear, I am not saying, "Look at my kid, ain't she great?" My view is quite the opposite. I firmly believe that with the right approach, *every* child can reach their maximum potential, from a reading standpoint, much faster and with much greater ease, by directly and adequately addressing some basic visual functions. The earlier the intervention occurs, the better. Visual processing skills *emerge* as a result of proper eye-teaming skills – so let us make sure they are solid!

I hope that once you have finished this book, you will realize how easy it is to unleash the visual potential of your child. Hopefully, all you then have to do is stand back, and let the flood gates open and watch your child thrive, and not just "survive," like so many kids are doing right now in our school system as evidenced by the skyrocketing rates of IEPs. In 2013, it was estimated that one in ten students had an IEP, but now it is closer to two in ten. This epidemic needs to be addressed.

"Education is not filling a pail,
but the lighting of a fire."

W. B. YEATS (IRISH POET)

BEGINNING TO SEE

WC MAPLES, O.D., FCOVD

Vision in Child Development: Pregnancy and Birth

Child development is a vital component of a full life. This process of development begins before birth and is also ongoing throughout life from conception until death. Both pregnancy and early child development are critical parts of the development of visual space.

Vision is significantly involved in the overall development of the individual throughout one's life, and vision development will start in the womb. The baby will meet obstacles on its developmental journey and may take other than typical routes to completion, but the process does not expire.

The time from conception to birth is the most critical time in a person's life, and conception is the most crucial moment of that time. When the sperm enters the egg, at that moment, every gene and chromosome that will be expressed within the individual is set. Genetics will mark the uppermost limit of what the person will eventually be able to achieve. Although this may set the upper limit of potential, the environment, and the actions within the environment will govern how closely the person will come to realize their potential.

An aspect of the genetic code is a timer that governs the rate that the child will mature. This "maturational clock" triggers when the individual child will be ready to perform a task such as sitting up or walking. Although there is some variation in the time an individual child will show a behavior, the species does show a normal range where a skill (milestone) is developed.

You are pregnant — what a gift. The child growing within is already well on his/her way to maturity. Just as previously stated conception is the most critical time in one's life. Why is this? As the sperm penetrates the egg, the genetic makeup of your child is determined. The biological gender is determined, and the overall potential of the child is set in place.

As the egg is fertilized, the maturational clock begins to tick. The fertilized egg begins a journey down the fallopian tube to embed itself in the wall of the uterus. The whole process from the last menstruation period to birth is ideally 280 days, ten lunar months or, 40 weeks.

During the first 12 weeks of pregnancy, all the organs and structures will be developed. It is the most critical time in a pregnancy. One must be particularly careful of the mother's health and particularly what the mother ingests. Alcohol, smoking, and recreational drugs are taboo. Follow your family doctor's advice as to any prescribed medications. If some unwanted influence (measles, drugs, etc.) is introduced, dire consequences can result. An example of unwanted interference in development would be substance abuse (fetal alcohol syndrome) or the Thalidomide children of the 1950s. This drug was given (mostly in Europe) to treat morning sickness, but it interfered with the long bone development of the baby in the first trimester.

Eye development starts by the 4th week of pregnancy. It begins by growing out of the tissue that is developing the brain. This eye development process will continue throughout the pregnancy and into the first few weeks after birth. The neurology of the eye is not considered to be fully developed until about 3 to 4 months *after* birth.

After the completion of the first trimester, the second trimester is about growth in new cells as well as an increase in the size of cells. The second trimester will be when the "baby bump" is seen; the mother begins to show. The chances of miscarriage are reduced dramatically. By the end of the second trimester, about 28 weeks, the baby may survive birth with modern medical care. However, delivery is by no means desirable until the full 40 weeks have been completed. In fact, being three weeks or more premature is associated with a significantly higher risk of developing a visibly turned eye.

Even though the retina of the eye will not be completely developed until after birth, the labyrinthine system (inner ear) and the eye muscles are beginning to work together long before birth. The eye muscles and the inner ears are neurologically linked very early in development. This means that when the baby, floating in the amniotic fluid, rolls right or left, the eyes move in the opposite direction so that the eyes and inner ears are functioning together at birth. Because of this, as well as for the overall health of the child, we recommend that the mother-to-be engages in a gentle exercise program that allows the developing baby to rock to and fro within the womb. Each movement will reinforce this labyrinthine/eye muscle coordination.

The third trimester is marked by the elaboration of all the muscles and nerves. The baby will already have been moving in the uterus. These movements are helping the child to develop the neurological patterns that will dictate the movement of the muscles at birth. Movement patterns are being established (primitive reflexes) essential to early survival and development of the newborn. The usual presence or absence of these reflexes is a very first indicator of problems.

Birth is the next most crucial time. A paper reported factors at birth that were significant indicators of eye and vision problems. Conditions that concern optometrists in the newborn/infant are various eye diseases that can cause blindness. These may include: ptosis (drooping eyelids), cataracts (cloudy eyes) and retinal diseases. Also, and much more prevalent are the three conditions of amblyopia (lazy eye), esotropia (crossed eye), and anisometropia (imbalance between the two eyes). The most significant factors reported in the study were if one or both parents had one of these conditions (genetic predisposition). This factor was almost ten times more likely to predict the child that would have an eye/vision condition. The second most significant factor was the mother's health during the pregnancy, specifically high blood pressure, six times more likely to have problems.

Other factors impacting eye/vision conditions were related to the birth process. These included: gender (boys more likely to have problems than girls), prematurity, low birth weight, and the use of supplemental oxygen at birth, or any systemic disease of the child were significant. If the child is born premature three weeks or more and/or with a birth weight of 5 lbs., 5 oz. or less, then their odds of eye-teaming issues is significantly increased. The nature of the birth process was also a factor. If the mother had a spontaneous vaginal delivery, the child was less likely to have vision problems. Likewise, if there was a forceps, vacuum-assisted or Caesarean section, the child was more likely to have a vision problem. It was further noticed in the paper that if the child had bouts of otitis media (middle ear infection), the child was likely to have more eye/vision problems.

The development of vision is a significant aspect of child growth and maturity. The eye and the visual process develop through defined milestones. These milestones are behaviors parents should observe at different stages of development to ensure optimal visual health. Actions by the parent to foster the child's visual and overall growth can assist in this overall development. Not experiencing a proper milestone may be detrimental to your child's development.

At birth, the baby moves. There are predictable movements in response to a stimulus (primitive reflexes), and there are also non-specific responses. If one pricks the newborn's arm with a pin, the whole baby will react. He will kick, flail his arms, and begin to cry, a whole-body reaction. These movements will become more discrete with development. Later if you prick the arm, they will likely respond by moving their arm, a more discrete movement based upon elaboration of their sensory development. The more mature the child becomes, the more discrete the ability to control their muscles and to show perceptual and cognitive awareness. As this phenomenon continues, primitive reflexes are being suppressed as an indication of the maturity of the person.

Many primitive reflexes will hopefully be suppressed with the maturation of the person. If these reflexes are not suppressed, this may indicate a neurological problem. Your pediatrician will be well versed in these reflexes. A few retained reflexes have been related to the development of vision and overall growth. These retained reflexes may be linked to inability to sit still, hyperactivity, the inability to focus, and subsequent poor academic performance once formal education is started. The most significant of these reflexes are the Moro reflex, asymmetric tonic neck, symmetric tonic neck, tonic labyrinthine reflex, and Galant reflex (spinal Galant).

The Moro reflex is a startle reflex. Quickly moving the child's head or a loud sound will cause the child's arms and legs to move up and out and then move to the center of the body, with the child subsequently crying. This is a response to grasp and hold the mother. This reflex relates to the bilateral integration of the muscle systems of the body as well as arousal.

The asymmetrical tonic neck reflex is easily recognizable in that the newborn's head will be turned to one side and the arm on that side will be extended. The other arm will be flexed as if he is a swordsman in the "fencing stance." This reflex is considered necessary for the development of the eye fixation, and is the genesis of eye-hand coordination.

The symmetric tonic neck reflex is not present at birth but appears around six months. If the baby is held so that they are facing the floor, the head is directed down toward the chest, the arms will pull together, and the legs will extend. Conversely, if the head is moved up, the arms will stretch, and the legs will contract. The reflex will later morph into crawling and walking.

A tonic labyrinthine reflex is present at birth. When the head is tilted back, the back will become rigid and arch while the legs extend. The arms and hands will tense and move toward the midline. This reflex is vital for the baby's future ability to stand against gravity. It also has implications in the development of eye muscle coordination, cognitive space development, and balance.

The Galant reflex is a motor response when one side of the spine is stimulated. The baby will move away from the stimulus. This movement is said to be present to assist the baby moving down the birth canal during birth. If it is retained, it is related to fidgeting and hyper-activity, especially when the child has to maintain contact between the lower back and a chair. They will often be much more settled for example on an exercise ball, which avoids contact with the lower back area.

It is essential to know that these reflexes are vital for the elaboration of movement and the eventual development of the perceptual/cognitive skill of spatial perception. All the mentioned reflexes, except for the symmetrical tonic neck, should be diminished or disappear by six months of age. As a corollary, eye muscle coordination, retinal development, eye focusing, and eye-teaming should all be present by four months of age. Especially, when the asymmetric tonic neck reflex disappears, one should see straight eyes. Up until that time, it is not unusual to see one of the baby's eyes turn in or out periodically. If this is not the occasion, take your child to a developmental/behavioral optometrist. The American Optometric Association has a program where an infant (up to 1 year) will be evaluated at no charge (Infantsee). This is a service the parent should avail themselves.

Pregnancy, the birth process , and the early development of the child is a critical aspect of what this child will become. We find that the development, however, has just begun and there are many more milestones as the child moves from infancy toward school age.

"Patrick, always remember that the bigger muscles teach the smaller muscles how to move. In vision therapy, always start where they are, and go where they ain't."

WC MAPLES TO PATRICK T. QUAID

THE MIRACLE OF VISION

GLEN T. STEELE, O.D., FCOVD, FAAO

"Vision is the FOUNDATION in the Process of Development Vision is the ROCK of Development."

Development is not a hobby. It is a vital component of a full life, and the process of development begins before birth. The process is ongoing throughout life from conception until death. As an optometrist, little can be done before birth regarding development. Since vision is significantly involved in overall development throughout the rest of one's life, there is much that an optometrist can do once the baby is born. The process of development does not expire. It will meet obstacles and may take other than typical routes to completion, but it does not expire.

Development is Active and Voluntary

Development does not happen in a vacuum or like a toy that you wind up and send on its way. Growth is an active process throughout life. For example, in vision, the development of "focusing" must be an active and voluntary process. It involves the coordination of all ocular functions in conjunction with many body functions. Ocular motility, binocular function, accommodation, and the ability to maintain these visual skills as the patient moves eyes to look are the basics of oculomotor control. Maintaining posture, position, and proper body movement are also involved in "focusing." All of these processes feed back and forth to each other – the vision process gives the body information about posture and positioning and the body posture and positioning give the visual process information about visual orientation. When these processes are in sync, everything works well. When they are not in sync, additional effort is required that limits the information to be gained from "focusing."

Vision and Development are Multifactorial

To quote S. P. Johnson in the chapter Development of the Visual System in Neural Circuit Development and Function in the Brain, 2013,

> "... because visual development stems from growth, maturation, and experience from learning and action; all happen simultaneously and all influence one another. Infants free of disability or developmental delay are born with a functional visual system that is prepared to contribute in important ways to learning, but incapable of perceiving objects in an adult-like fashion."

Vision is the Foundation Throughout the Process of Development

Vision development is the FOUNDATION in all aspects of vision assessment and care, including therapy. Vision becomes the ROCK and leader in all aspects of development. Vision D evelopment and Overall Development go hand in hand throughout life. All development is timeless and impacts every aspect of one's life. Changes in development lead to internal transformation and later to changes in individual function.

Arnold Gesell, M.D. was a pediatrician at the Yale Clinic of Child Development and later director of the Gesell Institute of Child Development founded by Louise Ames, PhD and Frances Ilg, M.D. Among his writings, Gesell authored; Vision: Its Development in Infant and Child. In this book, he provided a wonderful foundation for understanding the process of vision and how it develops. He linked this knowledge of the visual process with an increased in-depth understanding of overall development. Most importantly, he provided a guide for making observations of overall development through vision assessment and what can be done through the visual process to enhance overall development. Originally published in 1949, the third edition (2018) continues to support the concepts of Gesell's early research and writings.

Within VISION, Gesell laid the foundation for and introduced concepts that were later linked in his concepts of overall development. He did not think of eyes, refraction, or strabismus first. He looked for a deeper illumination of what a child uses vision for, what their focus is, and recognized that as the developing child's visual foundation becomes more complete, their potential for overall development is enhanced. This was previously noted in other Gesell works, (particularly Developmental Diagnosis – chapter 13 on Blindness) and an article entitled Infant Vision from Scientific American.

Many works of today continue to support these early observations amazingly captured on video throughout the process of development. When both doctor and caregiver actively seek to understand the process of development, the patient will be the recipients, and ultimately, the beneficiaries, of such care.

An example is a work done by Andrew Meltzoff and Rechele Brooks from the University of Washington. In their article, The Development of Gaze Following and It's Relation to Language; they noted that "... infants who had a correct gaze + simultaneous vocalization at 10-11 months understood significantly more words (337) than those who did not produce this act (194) at 18 months)."

The process of vision development begins well before birth, which is beyond the scope of this chapter. Once a healthy child is born, the process of developing vision starts almost immediately. While the visual process importantly is often referred to as a sensory process, the process begins as a motor process. The process starts with efforts to look. Where and how the developing child looks is determined by their innate curiosity. As they actively and more directly look, their sensory function works to identify and engage with the object long before hands can move to touch and feel. When the developing child begins to reach, the process of visually looking has been in place for three to four months. The process of looking develops more quickly and efficiently as parents and caregivers visually engage with the child.

The foundations of visual development in a healthy child appear to be very simple, yet they are very complex. Ocular motility is more than "following a target." It is the engagement of the child within their environment in developing the process of visually "simple eye reaching" (looking). The binocular function is more than alignment. It is the development of visually "reaching" with both eyes at the same place *at the same time.* Accommodation is more than focusing the eyes to make the object clear. It is the process of using reaching, alignment, and focusing in the process of identification. As the infant and young child develop more control of the foundational pieces of vision, the ability to identify comes more quickly and more efficiently.

The more effectively one can reach with vision, communication, taste, smell, and touch, the better the process of the overall development. The motor experiences must come first – the intention to accomplish. It is not the sensory experiences first. It is the motor experiences first, then the sensory experiences to identify. Look, then identify. The more intentional one looks, the more effective is the ability to use the sensory aspects of the visual system.

The Circle of Understanding

The Circle of Understanding is that close area within the developing child's ability to reach and explore. This begins as a small circular area within arm's reach in which the child can quickly and repeatedly reach and explore. They also "reach" with other processes such as olfactory (smell), gustatory (taste), kinesthesia (feel), and auditory (listen) to fully understand the object or situation.

Development is expanding the Circle of Understanding. Progress does not happen in a linear fashion or at the same time for everyone. Depending upon how and why they break through the Circle of Understanding, their world expands. The baby then begins to "focus" their interests formed as an outgrowth of their internal curiosity. Some find interest in the arts and others in the sciences. Some are active, and others are passive in development.

Often in the process of development, infants and young children do not have the curiosity to explore and may stay within their Circle of Understanding. A useful visual process stimulates moving and interacting with objects beyond the Circle of Understanding. Reaching beyond this small area is significant in exploring new objects and ideas even into adulthood. Development is so much more than looking internally or inward to themselves. It must involve looking externally and exploring beyond – looking versus seeing. As much as the child and adult may wish to explore a new concept, how they take the first step beyond their comfort zone may have its origins from very early in development. It becomes much easier to understand differences in life opportunities in highly successful people when one was considered an active learner and another a passive learner. Both are successful but in many different ways.

Vision must become the leader when engaging in activities beyond the Circle of Understanding. Not to diminish the sensory aspect of vision, but it can be severely limited if the motor is not capable. Looking – the motor aspect – must come first. "We look to see clearly, not BECAUSE we see clearly." One Fixates accurately in order to see clearly not because one sees clearly *

We connect by LOOKING and later recognize and connect through our other sensory processes.

Development is Intentional-Integrated-Interdependent

The more effectively we can reach with vision, communication, taste, smell, and touch, the better we become. The intentional motor experiences must come first – the intention to accomplish. It is not the sensory experiences first. It is the motor experiences first, then the sensory experiences to identify. Look then identify. The more intentional we look, the better we can use the sensory aspects.

The Process of Doing

"Book" education alone will not set the stage for a full life. The same is true for passive observation. The process to become effective must involve doing. Through doing, the infant and young child learn what works and what does not and how modifications affect the outcome. Kids will get into difficult situations, and it is more than parent coddling or "games" on their device that allows them to step forward in life. They must have had to DO ! Doing is the result of innate curiosity moving into action. Vision is a significant factor in planning the necessary work and developing the abilities to make it happen.

It is not about seeing, hearing, or any of the sensory aspects. What is important is first connecting and making connections through the motor aspects of human functions – and that comes through LOOKING, listening, feeling, tasting, smelling. All of these are action words that indicate motor action. We short-change the concept of development when we only consider the sensory aspects. This also includes individual curiosity, which is the initial stage behind the motor processes. Looking is the process of initiating actions and connections while sensory comes into play for recognition and redirection of our actions.

The Opportunistic Times in Development

What are opportunistic times in vision development and overall development? These are times where events typically happen without obstacles or delays. These are the best times for a new stage of development to originate based on the previous stages. If the foundation is appropriate and curiosity is present, the stage will progress as expected. However, each new stage also presents a disruption in function. This may lead to discovering new ways to approach development or incomplete development due to the obstacles present. In the latter case, typical development may not occur as expected. Although a developmental stage does not expire, it may be more difficult to move through ensuing stages without the appropriate foundation of the previous stage(s) or if the stage does not happen at the opportunistic time(s).

Patients do not typically "grow out of" a missed opportunistic time. Although opportunistic time frames do not expire, there may be limited abilities coming out of this stage. Due to the limited foundation provided, ensuing stages may be limited. Such patients will not usually demonstrate typical development, but it can be gained with a timeline correction or other intervention(s).

Opportunistic stages and incomplete stages do not expire. They may become limited and more difficult to work through, but they do not expire. If a stage is not completed within the opportunistic time(s), the patient will not/may not have the foundation for ensuing stages until correction or appropriate intervention takes place. In this case, the function will be limited, but the opportunity has not expired. As these children have missed the opportunistic stages of development, more aggressive management will usually be indicated.

Disrupted Development and Undirected Recovery

During development, disruptions come from many sources and happen over time or suddenly. Parents do the best they can to avoid disruptions, but they will always happen. Accidents and illness are the primary disruptions, but they may also include life changes such as parents moving to a new city or even having the support of only one parent. Without proper support, recovery may be undirected and leave the developing child in a state of confusion. This confusion results in withdrawing back into a smaller Circle of Understanding and limiting development.

Parents should not wait until there is a problem to solve or a barrier to remove before seeking intervention. Recovery from disruption progresses much more quickly when the patient makes an outward move through the "reaches." Most therapies are designed to initiate that change, and more. If the patient does not make the move to LOOK , the sensory only aspects will be reinforced until it becomes a pattern leading to a diagnosis. Treatment may be short term, but when built on the process of development as the FOUNDATION, the outcome becomes more like typical development.

"All anyone can learn is their next step. Skip that step and learning ceases. Find that step, and there is no telling what might happen."

UNKNOWN

READ ME A STORY

Having someone read to us is a vital step in acquiring literacy. It allows you to know what the word should sound like, regardless of the spelling of the word. However, I have learned that the key to efficient reading is being able to remember what the word looks like, even if it is not spelled how it sounds. This is often the case in the English language.

This, in essence, allows rapid recognition or "smoothness of decoding," leading to reading fluency. The English language, in particular, is notorious for not sounding like it is spelled. Just think of the words yacht, knight, and knot to name a few. Of note, even though only 15-20% of words are deemed "sight words" in the English language, i.e., they do not follow any known phonetic rules, these sight words occupy up to 80% of written print on a page! On their own, these are words that do not convey much meaning, in and of themselves but are required to "connect the text." Words like "they, who, should, could" for example. Think about the word "there," or is it "their" or is it "they're?" They all sound the same, yet are spelled differently. They also have completely different meanings, depending on the context. These are mostly the words that messed me up as a child. I could often figure out how the words sounded, but could not for the life of me recall how they looked.

Think about the rules then that we give children, such as, "I before E except after C." Then do a "Feisty heist on a beige neighbor." Yes, these words all violate that "rule." Even the word "science" violates that rule! It is ironic that even if we learn all known phonetic rules, we still would be unable to decode less than 50% of written print on a page. I am not saying that phonetics are not useful - far from it. If a child spells "future," with p's and q's, the child may have phonetic awareness issues and may require intervention. They do not understand how sound and letters go together. However, most of the children we see in our clinic for reading and spelling issues tend to have a powerful phonetic spelling tendency. They will tend to spell yacht, as "yot" and will spell most words as they sound, which usually results in an incorrect spelling in the English language. What therefore continually confuses me, is that if a child "misspells words but spells them how they sound," how will their reading benefit from "tutoring and phonetic awareness work"? How will this help? They already spell how things sound. Making them "more phonetically aware," is likely not very useful, if the goal is to have them remember what the words look like.

It makes much more sense to work on their visual memory skills and help them to remember what the symbols look like, regardless of how they sound. Visual memory is a critical skill that is rarely discussed in the "Reading Remediation" world. It is not often mentioned in the world of eye-care either. Being able to read efficiency (fluently) and decode text quickly, in essence, requires a seldom-referenced skill called "Selective Inattention," or as I prefer to call it, Divided Attention.

Let us talk about the term "Selective Inattention," first of all. It refers to one's ability to look at a word and understand its meaning, as it is properly pronounced (said out loud), regardless of how it looks and would be pronounced phonetically (sounded out). Look at the word "station." Now, sound it out as it is spelled. It sounds odd, "stat" and "ion," but when we look at the word, we do not think about this. We automatically know that it just "sounds differently" than it is spelled. We know from prior experience that it sounds more like "stashon" and read it as such, regardless of spelling.

How did we learn to do this? Over time, the more a word is used by the general population, the more its sounds tend to become relaxed or clipped, to be more suitable for oral use. The written word, however, does not change. Therefore over time, the language starts to sound quite different from the printed word. Some languages are much more prone to this mismatch. English is a prime example. Other languages, such as my wife's first language, Turkish, are derived from the Western alphabet and is very phonetically based. Turkish words are typically spelled how "they sound" to the ear, and are therefore much easier to learn. I also learned Gaelic in Ireland, which is almost as difficult as English. So, the reason we say that "Selective Inattention" is required to read, is that you have to be able to accept the difference between the printed words visually while accepting that it will be pronounced differently. This process just happens in fluent readers. So in children when it does not "just happen," we have to ask – what is going wrong?

Usually, one of two things has become an issue. It could be that their phonetics are off, causing the child to spell a word completely wrong. It might even bear no similarity to how it sounds, (i.e., spelling "future," not as "fucher," but with random letters included in the attempt.) This problem is termed a "Dysphonetic Issue " in that the child does not understand how letters and sounds even go together in the first place. In a case like this, we would usually refer the child out to a hearing professional and a speech and language pathologist (SLP), to look strongly at whether there is a primary hearing issue and/or phonetic awareness issue that needs to be addressed first.

In our clinic, our patients usually do not follow this pattern. Children that are brought to us for help, usually struggle with another issue. They also misspell words but use letters that reflect how the words truly sound. In other words, these children are phonetically aware and can hear how the word is spoken but do not remember how to spell them correctly. So it only stands to reason that the issue cannot be a phonetic one. The main point in these cases, termed, "Dyseidetic Reading Difficulties " is the failure of visual memory mechanisms. A topic rarely, if ever, touched on in reading-difficulty conversations. The lack of awareness of the importance of visual memory skill continues to baffle me. Visual memory is the end result of a properly developed and functioning visual system. Visual memory is the ability to *accurately recall what has been seen*. If one cannot remember what the word looks like, that is when the child will default into "sounding it out."

I was fortunate enough to have parents who read to me almost every night as a child, and an older brother who selflessly helped me with my homework, including French and Gaelic. I struggled for twelve years through English and Gaelic lessons, and also for six years with French in high school. Gaelic, of course, is mandatory in the Republic of Ireland, where I grew up. I am proud to have learned my native tongue, but the fact that I was wrestling with a visual issue and having to handle three languages did not help. The selfless act of my brother reading to me regularly is a debt I will never be able to repay. It gave me the invaluable gift of being able to appreciate how words properly sound. I still believe to this day, that my parents and my brother's help were the main reason I coped, despite being plagued with both a stammer and numerous visual issues.

What is very clear is this. Read to your children when they are young. Not only will you help their literacy and visual skills later on, you will also share the many adventures to be found in a great story, fun poetry, and tall tales. Those moments will form a special bond between you and your child that will last a lifetime!

"Anyone who thinks the art of conversation is dead ought to tell a child to go to bed."

ROBERT GALLAGHER

SEEING YOUR MEMORIES

What exactly is Visual Memory?

Visual Memory is the ability of the brain to recall what has been seen. When you think of a word such as "America" or "Canada" and then try to spell them backward, you try to *picture or visualize* the word in your head. Most of us do not sound it out in our head or try to spell the word the way it sounds.

This reality makes sense when we have 1.22 million ganglion cells per optic nerve and only 30,000 ganglion cells per ear. Ganglion cells are akin to wires connecting an organ to the brain. So, using this analogy, if I had a large cable and a small cable coming into my TV, and my TV was malfunctioning, I would look at the large cable first. Now, this does not mean that the small cable is unimportant, but it makes more sense to check the larger cable first. This appears to be occurring in most cases where children are having difficulty reading. Visual Memory tends to be the large cable that gets ignored or overlooked.

As an aside, help is often given to children with these issues, typically in schools, technologically. Computers and iPads are increasingly used to aid students who struggle with reading paper-based print. Research found in the International Journal of Educational Research has proven, that comprehension using paper-based print revealed significantly better comprehension rates, compared to the same information read on a computer screen. Clinically, and personally, I agree. As a struggling student myself, I always found paper-based reading easier than screen based reading. Most of my patients confirm this too.

Visual memory is also re-enforced by simply writing things down!

When I used to study in Optometry school, I would record the lectures on a Dictaphone (yes, I am older!). Then at night I would go home and write out notes based on the recording and my chicken scratches. I firmly think that this approach re-enforced visual memory as I am not only listening again to the material, but the act of writing it out is again re-enforcing the visual imagery of the wording and ideas. In fact, I used a lot of acronyms to allow me to *access* other memories. The funny thing is, when I picture the acronym (even now), I can easily visualize the page on which I wrote it. My memory includes the red letters I had written for the acronym's capital letters.

Visual-motor, (i.e., "writing") when combined with intact visual memory skills, is even more powerful as a memory aid. Research has shown that looking at a paper page gives about 30% better comprehension than the same material presented on a computer screen. I would bet that if you took the same material and wrote parts of it out by hand, then the retention would increase dramatically - again another level. The big idea here is that the visual memory skills are intact in the first place. This is the key.

Several papers have shown that measuring visual memory alone as a skill is highly predictive of reading failure or success in 3rd to 6th grade and also a strong predictor of mathematics skills. This makes perfect sense, as the child who can "picture the multiplication tables" also does not have to count on their fingers!

In our clinics, after having treated the underlying eye-teaming issues, we use Visual Memory techniques, with a list of 100 words that make up about 60% of all written print on an average page. We then move the child through the "Fry word list" (https://tinyurl.com/quaid-fry-ky) which has 100 words per grade from grade 1 the whole way to grade 10. This list is used in the visual rehabilitation of children with reading-based learning issues to great effect. Initially, it is introduced to build their confidence, as many of these kids have developed the "failure syndrome ," of giving up before they even try. We often hear after they quickly disengage, "Well, there you go, another thing I cannot do." The most rewarding challenge in our Optometric Vision

Therapy Clinic is to find the correct point, where children are succeeding, but are not bored or frustrated by having the level of therapy too high or too low.

The brain always craves constant and consistent input. A high level of visual performance, of course, is hard to achieve if there is fluctuating vision or intermittent double vision. These issues will cause the print to come "in and out of focus" in addition to potentially also seeing two words. Just think about this analogy, using two televisions. The first option is for you to watch a movie on a color TV. However, the channel is not exactly tuned in and is "coming in and out" of the channel. The second option is a crystal clear and consistent signal, but on a black and white TV. Which one would you pick to watch the film? The brain always chooses consistency over inconsistency, so most, if not all of us, would lean towards wanting the black and white, clear option. Now take this analogy to our visually developing brain as infants. The brain craves visual input consistency, and in fact, this is important for consistent visual neural pathways to form.

This principle can be summarized in what is known as Hebb's law; "Nerves that fire together, wire together." Dr. Donald Olding Hebb was a Canadian psychologist with a specific interest in how the brain learns. I would respectfully include the word "consistently," into his law, to read, "Nerves that consistently fire together, consistently wire together."

Why is inconsistent visual input detrimental to visual memory? If the nerves do not fire consistently, the opposite may happen. The brain will likely suppress or shut down the pathway in question if consistent firing is not happening. This makes sense, as the brain cannot make sense of the input if it is not consistent.

So, let us get back to connecting the dots in terms of reading. If one's visual input is not consistent, (i.e., blurry, then clear and/as double, then single, as tracking is off), this will result in the brain actively avoiding processing visual information. The brain not only loses this visual input but also loses the ability to further its neural maturity level.

If the hardware is off, the software will fail to develop. This lack of proper visual development is a significant issue since at least 40% of the brain's neural machinery is visual. In educational circles, teachers use data on dyseidetic errors (letter reversals, word reversals etc.) and use these pieces of evidence to convince parents there is a concern. The underlying cause of such dyseidetic reading issues, however, needs an even deeper focus.

Tragically, vision is often incorrectly simplified to "20/20" on a wall-based eye chart. The funny thing is, we don't read 6m (20 feet) away from the text, as we typically do during a routine eye exam. We usually read around 40cm (16 inches) away. Humans need to converge their eyes in order to read (i.e., pull them inwards), and we need to move them from side to side, while in a united position. This critical visual skill is called tracking or saccadic skills. (Saccadic is from the French verb, *saccader,* meaning to jump. i.e., eye jumps!) This equisitely complex eye-teaming task can very quickly go off the rails with even a minor disruption. It is usually quite easy to get 20/20, even with significant eye-teaming issues, as clearly shown in a publication by our own group in 2013. Published data showed that 14 out of 15 oculomotor (i.e., eye-teaming) skills examined were significantly impaired in a reading-difficulty group of children, compared to the controls (those children with no reading difficulties) in the study. The astonishing thing was that the ability of both groups to read the eye chart at a distance was almost indistinguishable, with most still seeing "20/20."

How ironic, that the one tool school nurses and eye doctors use for visual screening of students is actually of no value whatsoever in predicting reading ability. The good news is that there are at least 14 other visual skills that are highly useful in predicting reading ability. This is especially true when combined with a metric of visual memory skills.

As I've said, given the visual issues that I had growing up, I much preferred to be read to, instead of having to read myself. In hindsight now, of course, this makes perfect sense to me. I just preferred to avoid using my visual system. For the longest time, I wondered if there was something wrong with my eyes. As it turned out, I was correct, just not in an "eye-chart sense." It was really the brain's ability to control the eyes that was the issue. The eyes were *physically* healthy.

Over many years of telling my story to the parents of my pediatric patients, they have asked me to write this book. They were encouraged to see significant improvement in the academic progress of many of these children. By treating their visual issues thoroughly beyond "20/20," we have made a difference in their lives.

"Memory is the diary that we all carry about with us."

OSCAR WILDE

ALPHABET SOUP

English? It's Greek to me - or is that Latin or French? The many streams of languages that combine into what we now call English are elegant, sophisticated, diverse, and full of history. However, English, in particular, is not easy on the eyes.

So, I am going to make the case that the English language and certain symbols in particular in our alphabet are indeed not friendly to the visual system. In fact, given the amount of optical hardware and software required to be intact, to allow reading to occur, I am surprised that *more* kids do not have issues!

To explain this thoroughly, I have to take you on a short journey of the visual system and how it functions. This overview will help you understand and set the stage for the more detailed discussion of the visual hardware and software systems involved. Let's start with the basic concept of the brain and the eyes.

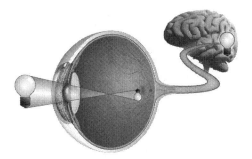

With vision, it is not just about an image being projected onto a retina. The brain has to make sense of that image. It stands to reason then, that any visual issues with the eyes affect how the brain is able to process that visual information. This is also a two-way street. Any damage to the brain would also likely change how our eyes function together. The brain and the eyes have a reciprocal agreement. The brain agrees to believe what the eyes see, and in exchange, the eyes agree to move to observe what interests the mind.

Now, let us take this engineering-like analogy to another level. The brain craves consistency. If it gets inconsistent information from any sensory source, it is likely to suppress it or shut down that pathway. Alternately, if the signal from a given pathway is consistent, the brain is very likely to use that pathway more frequently and also build on it over time. This makes sense in general.

Below is an image of what looks like a complex circuit diagram, but it is actually quite simple. The circle on the left (EYES) is the hardware of our visual system. Items such as eye-teaming, convergence, tracking ability, and image clarity come into play here. The bigger box is the brain. Within the brain are two circles, one representing STM (Short Term Memory), and the other representing LTM (Long Term Memory).

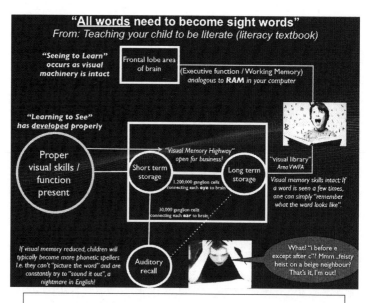

The left circle on the image above represents the eyes. Intact and properly functioning visual system. Visual Memory highway is "open for business."

Now, here is the fun part. I have also drawn smaller rectangular box at the top, representing our brain's frontal lobe. This primarily serves as your ability to "think on the fly." I have put this outside of the memory center, even though they are connected because I believe for the purpose of this discussion, they should be considered separately.

When I think of the frontal lobe of the brain, I always think about the donkey from the movie Shrek! The frontal lobe is the part of the brain that always tries to jump in and help (i.e., picture donkey jumping up and down saying, "Pick me, Pick me!") when another part of the brain is not doing its job properly. However, the frontal lobe should be free for the minute to minute attending. We often use terms like Executive Function or Working Memory in these situations, but in fact, I like to use the term Attention. When we say, "Pay attention." what exactly do we mean? Where are we "paying it from" exactly? That is an interesting notion. Of course, we need to know if the "reservoir" that we are drawing from is full or empty because if it is empty, we are not able to pay anything from an empty reservoir.

In the act of spelling, think about the name of the country or city in which you live and spell that word out loud. You will find that to be an easy task. Now, try it again but this time, spell it backwards and then notice the difference. I'm sure you will see that forwards is easy but backward is much harder. More than likely, you had to picture the word "in your head." This is why you probably looked into space somewhere or looked up and perhaps to the right, to help you visualize the word. Welcome to the world of visual memory. If the "eyes" circle has issues (i.e., the hardware) then the visual memory "highway" fails to develop. This only leaves the auditory pathway, which has a fraction of neuron bandwidth compared to the visual system.

This visual memory skill is your ability to recall sequences of symbols (eidetic memory), which is important for spelling. Visual memory is one's ability to recall what has been seen. This concept is critical in order to understand what this whole book addresses. Ohio State University research has shown that visual memory is a very strong predictor of success in BOTH reading and mathematics. As an aside, it is usually the first to go and the last to recover in our concussion patients also, hence why they are all complaining of short-term memory issues. That is another topic for another book by itself.

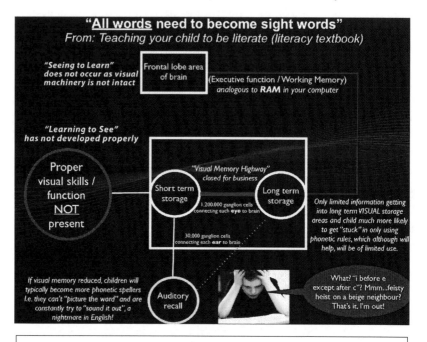

"All words need to become sight words"
From: Teaching your child to be literate (literacy textbook)

"Seeing to Learn" does not occur as visual machinery is not intact

Frontal lobe area of brain

(Executive function / Working Memory) analogous to **RAM** in your computer

"Learning to See" has not developed properly

Proper visual skills / function **NOT** present

"Visual Memory Highway" closed for business

Short term storage

1,200,000 ganglion cells connecting each **eye** to brain

Long term storage

Only limited information getting into long term VISUAL storage areas and child much more likely to get "stuck" in only using phonetic rules, which although will help, will be of limited use.

30,000 ganglion cells connecting each **ear** to brain

If visual memory reduced, children will typically become more phonetic spellers I.e. they can't "picture the word" and are constantly try to "sound it out", a nightmare in English!

Auditory recall

What? "i before e except after c"? Mmm...feisty heist on a beige neighbour? That's it, I'm out!

Offline and improperly functioning visual system results in the Visual Memory Highway going offline. Now the only pathway available is auditory. Hence the phonetic spelling patterns.

So, let us talk about the ramifications of visual memory going offline, as shown in the diagram above. The eyes, (hardware), circle is now offline, as there is, for example, an oculomotor issue. This could be one or more of the at least 17 visual areas that we can assess. Now, if the hardware goes offline, you notice that the "VM HWY" (Visual Memory Highway) has now started to break down. This makes sense, as the brain will not tolerate inconsistent visual input. If, for example, a word you are looking at is clear one moment but blurry the next, or single one moment and all mashed together, or doubled the next, the brain soon stops attending to that information. A child dealing with these types of issues cannot be expected to be successful at remembering what a word looks like under these conditions. In other words, visual memory, the Queen Bee, fails.

Now add into this alphabet soup, the fact that the English language has many, many words that are not spelled as they sound. If you think about it, we usually remember or memorize what the word sounds like, even though it is not how it is spelled. A child with a visual issue can not do this and is put at a real disadvantage as a result.

When a parent brings their child to my clinic stating that their child has "reading issues," my first job is to determine whether the source of the issue is rooted in visual memory or not. I ask the child to spell some words and determine if they are spelling them the way they sound or if they are throwing in random letters that make no sense at all. After that, we can talk about specific standardized tests. It is as simple as that; if the child spells words the way they sound, they have a visual memory issue. In these cases, it is much more likely that they cannot recall what the word looks like. After all, if they cannot picture the words, their only other option is to try and spell the words the way they sound. If the reading issue is not involving visual memory, and the child is spelling words with random, nonsensical letters that do not even make phonetic sense, then the child does not understand how sounds and letters go together. Phonetic issues are when the child does not understand how letter and sounds go together. So, the first step is to decide which problem they have. Accurate assessment must occur in order for effective intervention to be prescribed.

Sadly, this simple step is not often undertaken before remediation takes place. Often it is assumed that the child needs more tutoring and requires phonetic awareness work with a Speech and Language Pathologist (SLP). This approach will indeed be highly effective *if* the child has mainly a phonetic awareness issue. However, if they have a visual memory issue, which in essence would be rooted in a visual problem, tutoring and SLP work will likely not help, or at best have very limited effectiveness. After all, how does teaching a child more phonics, who already spells phonetically, help? One needs to address the visual memory issue first.

It makes much more sense in cases with underlying visual issues to address the underlying oculomotor (i.e., visual hardware) problem initially. Then deal with the visual processing issues. The ultimate goal is to improve visual memory to permit visual images to be stored for future recall.

So as a parent, or an educator, if you see a persistent phonetic spelling pattern in the child avoiding reading and writing, this is an outright clue. Does the child prefer to be read to rather than reading themselves? Does he or she prefer to tell you a story rather than write one out? This tells you they are setting up their environment to avoid using their visual system.

Another very important clue is the fact that noise will knock them off their game very quickly. If a patient has a visual issue, they will tend to be more auditory learners than visual learners. Therefore, if there is background noise, it will affect an auditory learner in more dramatic ways, than a visual learner, as they are primarily leaning on their hearing, as opposed to their vision.

Now, let us focus a little more on visual memory and where in the brain the image of a word is stored. This visual library, so to speak, is where we tap into when we are trying to picture a word *visually*. There is a part of the brain called VWFA, which stands for Visual Word Form Association. This is our "visual library." Here, we store sight words (or as SLP's call them, "jail words.") These are words that in essence do not follow phonetic rules (so are put in jail) and "we just have to know how to spell them." Ultimately, all words have to become sight words to allow fluent reading and comprehension to occur. Area VWFA is the last visual area before visual information is combined with auditory information. This integration between hearing what the word sounds like and what the word looks like happens in a part of the brain called the Planum Temporale, or as I like to call it the "where-we-make-the-sound-and-image-of-the-word-match" center.

A large proportion of the neurons in the area VWFA, are in fact what we call, Mirror Neurons. The term is used for visual neurons that are designed to look at an object from different perspectives but continue to treat it as the "same object." Think of your car at home from different angles. You, of course, recognize that it is the same object regardless of the viewpoint you from which you see it. This seems like a minor point but just imagine what kind of world we would encounter, if every time we looked at an object from a different angle, it seemed like a new object to our brain! That would be so confusing. As most VWFA visual neurons are Mirror Neurons, they are used heavily in visual memory overall.

As a species, we have been reading for a relatively short time in the great span of history. If you think of human history as a day, we have only been reading for the last 30 seconds or so. Using our eyes to read is not something we did until *very* recently. So what did VWFA neurones do before we read? The answer is intriguing. Neurons in area VWFA are also used for facial recognition. Faces are reasonably symmetrical about the vertical axis; draw a line vertically down the center of someone's face from the top of the head to the chin and most are symmetrical, but not the horizontal axis, from one ear to the other.

An interesting connection here is that when children are learning to read, there is an obvious difficulty with deciphering, "b's and d's," and also, "p's and q's." If a small "b" is simply the same image of a "d" backward, what would mirror neurones say? YES – they are the same! To differentiate between the same letters flipped around quickly, we have to *inhibit normal mirror neurone activity*! That is quite a statement.

Mirror neuron activity can be appropriately suppressed for most people learning to recognize letters quickly when all other visual hardware and software is functioning correctly. When there is a visual issue, however, the brain fails to inhibit the normal mirror neuron tendencies, resulting in persistent letter reversals on the familiar letters, (p, q, b, d), as seen especially on written output.

This, by the way, is also a great argument to continue to teach cursive writing! After all, a cursive p, q, b, and d, are visually not flipped images. Compare that to the "ball and a stick" images of lower case printed b, d, p and q. These are much easier to flip without realizing. I saw this in my daughter. When learning to print, she picked up all the other letters very quickly. However, it took 3-4 months longer to get consistent accuracy with the b, d, p, and q, lower case letters.

This brings us back then to the interesting diagnosis of dyslexia, a term that usually rouses heated debate between visually trained professionals and phonetically trained professionals. At present, it is widely held that dyslexia is purely a phonetic issue. I would add to that statement the caveat, "It depends."

I struggle with the term dyslexia in the first place. It vaguely suggests that a child does not read very well, gets persistent reversals of letters and spelling sequences. However, it rarely pinpoints the problem. Developmentally, children diagnosed with dyslexia are generally fine.

A common test for dyslexia is the DST test (Dyslexia Screening Test). It is a commercially available test that has been used for decades by Developmental Optometry/Neuro-Optometry, as well as Speech and Language Pathology. It is used to determine whether a child's challenge is primarily "Can I remember how the word looks?" versus "Can I put sounds and letter sequences together properly?" It is simply a performance index in both "Visual Memory Ability" (Dyseidetic Score) and "Phonetic Awareness Ability" (Dysphonetic Score.)

The British Dyslexia Association (www.bdadyslexia.org.uk) has just recently added that a visual questionnaire and a thorough visual skills assessment be completed prior to booking any assessment with them, as any visual difficulties need to be explored in full before an assessment. They go on to state that given how common these visual issues are that if they are not ruled out prior to their assessment, the assessment may need to be stopped on their end. This is quite the statement and I sincerely applaud this approach. Visual difficulties must be ruled in or out early in such cases.

The word dyslexia comes from the Germanic term "dys," meaning "difficult," and the Greek term "lexis," referring to "for speech." However, dyslexia is usually identified as a reading issue, not a difficulty for speech. The term was originally coined in the late 19th century by a German ophthalmologist – an eye doctor! He thought that his patients, despite their reading challenges, had perfect vision. Why? He was only using as his measurement of normal vision, the "20/20" on the eye chart. He was using the one vision metric that we now know is inaccurate for differentiating between efficient readers and poor readers!

Now, this particular ophthalmologist was correct in mentioning in his writings that dyslexia appears to be an issue with the brain. However, research had not yet revealed how much of the brain was visual machinery outside of "20/20" in the central 4-6 degrees of the otherwise massive visual field of about 180° degrees (plus) horizontally and 160° vertically.

The question to be answered for the parent who brings their child to my clinic with "dyslexia" is this. Does your child have a visual issue and/or a poor understanding of how sound and letters go together?

When diagnosing dyslexia, the DSM-V clearly states: "The individual's difficulties must not be better explained by developmental, neurological, sensory (vision or hearing) or motor disorders." This is in agreement with the research. In fact, research published in 2018 showed that 79% of children with developmental dyslexia have significant visual problems and also just as shockingly, 33% of the control group in the study also had significant visual issues. Keep in mind that this research was published by PhDs both from medicine and optometry and was published in the medical journal JAMA. (Follow this ink https://tinyurl.com/quaid-jama for the article.) COVD International also has a white paper position out on the link (https://tinyurl.com/covd-dyslexiapdf) between visual concerns and dyslexia making a thorough visual assessment an obvious critical piece to any child labelled with this term. Despite often "seeing 20/20", visual skills issues are very common in dyslexia cases and need to be addressed.

I want you to also think about another fascinating finding. It is possible to be dyslexic in one language and not in another! In Turkey, dyslexia is not found commonly in native Turkish-speaking children until they begin to learn English. This is because the Turkish language is primarily a phonetic language. It is written precisely as spoken and spoken exactly as written. A journal article published by Butterworth and Tang in Nature looked at the prevalence of dyslexia in the Chinese language compared to English. They found that English speakers have a six times higher rate of dyslexia than Chinese speakers. The title of the write up in the Guardian newspaper describing this research, was, "Dyslexia has a language barrier." This makes sense as Chinese is a pictorial language and has no symbols, that when reversed, have a different meaning. In other words, Chinese is friendly to the visual system's natural strengths and also does not contain symbols that violate normal mirror neurone activity in area VWFA.

In English, we must remember what the words look like - even if they sound different from how they look visually. Visual memory and visual skills are critical and a largely overlooked aspect of the reading acquisition process. They are required to be in place and intact for effortless and automatic decoding of text to emerge. This is precisely what Optometric Vision Therapy in our clinic aims to address, the visual skills deficits that impede visual memory emergence and ultimately, our ability to thrive in the educational arena. After all, most education is based on the premise that what I show you today, you can remember tomorrow. If this mechanism fails, the learning process comes to a grinding halt.

"The principle goal of education in the schools should be creating men and women who are capable of doing new things, not simply repeating what other generations have done."

JEAN PIAGET

ADHD – DIAGNOSIS OR SYMPTOM?

What if Attention Deficit status is a *symptom* and not a diagnosis? After all, there is no blood test, imaging, or objective diagnostic test for this label. Why would we not ask, "If a child cannot *attend* (pay attention), let us find out why not?"

The phrase "simultaneously visually attend" refers to the ability to look in one place, but at the same time be visually attending somewhere else. As an example from the hearing world, imagine you are having a conversation with someone. At the same time, someone else in the room is having a separate discussion and mentions your name! You proceed to *pretend* to be listening to the original conversation, but now you are trying to ATTEND, or listen in, on the other conversation. This is a great example of Divided Auditory Attention. I am hearing from one direction but ATTENDING to a completely different sound source. Visually Divided Attention is very similar. You are pointing your eyes at a particular spot, but you are visually ATTENDING to a different area. At the core of many eye tracking issues and visual processing issues is poor divided visual attention skills. This is often the child who reacts to *anything* moving in the peripheral vision field which can look like "inability to maintain concentration" overall.

Treat the source of the problem rather than just hoping that symptoms get better. Avoid a misdiagnosis and end up medicating the wrong symptom. *Perhaps* it is a visual eye-teaming issue. Given that at least 40% of the entire brain is used for visual processing and 5 out of the 9 Diagnostic and Statistical Manual (DSM) symptoms are identical to eye-teaming issues, this is a reasonable approach.

I resist labeling a child with a vague "attentional issue," based on a handful of questionnaires. Instead, I recommend doing a proper work-up to determine if there are any underlying functional issues that are contributing to the problem. This is especially so given strong evidence from a study published by researchers from Princeton, Cornell University and the University of Toronto showing little evidence of academic gains with medication. Their conclusion at the last sentence says it all. They state "Our results suggest that observers of the large increases in the use of medication for ADHD in Canada, the USA and other countries are right to be concerned." There is a level one evidence trial, however; showing that eye-teaming issues can be effectively treated (CITT study). This has also been shown to result in academic benefit. It is at least a possibility to consider.

There are literally dozens of eye-teaming tests (i.e., depth perception, convergence, near-far focussing tests, etc.), that can be done to assess if the visual system is abnormal. These tests go far beyond the "20/20 is normal" assumption. A little known fact is that more than 60% of ADHD symptoms are identical to the symptoms of one common eye-teaming issue, called Convergence Insufficiency (CI.) CI is the difficulty of the eyes to sustain an inward posture. This ability is obviously important for reading! In the general population, the incidence of CI is about 3-4%, at least as high as 8% in some studies. ADHD cases have documented incidence of 15.9%. Remember, we are only talking here about *one* eye condition (CI). Many more could be involved.

We all would benefit from more conversations regarding the common symptoms of other conditions similar to ADHD. If these labels were in vogue when I was a kid, I would likely have been on the medications. These medications have side effects. When speaking to children in our clinic who get off the medications and those that are old enough to verbalize it, they report chronic sleeplessness, appetite suppression, and weight loss while on the medication. They also report feeling numb and "zoned out." Children have developing brains. Let's be certain that we have a clear diagnosis that rules out the other possibilities before we medicate.

There are cases, of course, where medicating is appropriate - but only after proper diagnostic work-up. In my opinion, ADHD should be a diagnosis of exclusion, a last resort. This is a diagnosis that is only considered after all the neuro-sensory possibilities have been ruled out.

In the most recent version of the ADHD guidelines, vision is not even discussed in terms of the eye chart, let alone eye-teaming problems. This misses a crucial piece of the puzzle. The research shows undeniable links between poor attention, reading issues and oculomotor dysfunction. Several peer-reviewed publications from both medicine and optometry have shown that attentional issues overlap significantly with visual issues, in terms of symptomatology. Given that ADHD/ADD is primarily a symptom-based diagnosis, this connection should be highlighted to a much greater extent to parents and educators.

If a child has to work harder than their peers to maintain clarity and fusion (i.e., not to see blurred and/or double) when reading, they will disengage faster from the task. These behaviours then, mimic ADHD behaviours, in terms of symptomatology and the confusion in diagnosis begins.

Before defaulting to an ADHD diagnosis, we need to go beyond the routine eye examination for eye disease and significant glasses prescriptions. The routine eye examination is vital, but we also need to ask for a full visual skills and visual processing assessment, ideally, by an eye doctor with extra training in the areas such as a board certification and/or fellowship training. (FCOVD - see www.covd.org) These doctors have a specific interest in the field of oculomotor dysfunction and visual processing dysfunction. They are able to test and treat in-depth issues, ranging from tracking dysfunction to subtle eye misalignments. It is imperative for all of us to recognize the link between attention and proper visual function and visual processing abilities. Our children deserve better.

"Truth passes through three stages.
First, it is ridiculed. Second, it is violently opposed.
Third, it is accepted as self-evident."

ARTHUR SCHOPENHAUER

COLLABORATION & COORDINATION

DR. DEBORAH ZELINSKY

Families of children who have difficulties with learning, behavior, eating or sleeping, are frequently offered copious testing and therapy options which may not always be sufficient or effective in pinpointing the source(s) of the problem.

Understanding the myriad of ways in which the body reacts and responds to both internal and external stimulation is a critical first step in effectively treating a child's disorder. To achieve maximal improvement, we must collaborate and coordinate treatment and testing with other healthcare professionals. There is a spectrum of methods available in the traditional fields of occupational, physical, speech therapies as well as in newer fields, such as reflex integration, Feldenkrais, cognitive restructuring and neuro-optometry.

A common example would be a child who has difficulty reading. Typically, the child would be offered a conventional eyesight evaluation without necessarily testing two other crucial components:

1. Determining how the child's peripheral awareness is used in conjunction with central eyesight and
2. Assessing how the child's auditory system (used in phonemic awareness and decoding) is interacting with the visual system (used in learning sight words).

Answers to those questions may elicit valuable information that otherwise might not be uncovered.

A child with sensory-processing dysfunction might be prescribed occupational therapy without being given a comprehensive vision and/or hearing evaluation. If a child's visual and auditory functions are indeed evaluated, these tests may be performed separately, rather than in an integrated fashion. The tests should not be done separately, since eyesight and hearing pathways are regularly used together. Recent research has shown that the more stable the link between auditory and visual systems, the better and more efficient the person's spatial awareness. Since 2014, many functional studies have demonstrated linkages between auditory and visual spatial perception. Researchers at Duke University have shown structurally that when the eyes move, the eardrums oscillate — even without any sound. In fact, the more the gaze shifts, the more the eardrum oscillates. Eyes and ears must be looked at as a team.

Although most children in America receive standard vision screenings at school, other testing may be more useful in detecting eye/ear integration problems in certain cases. There are multiple visual systems that can impact a child's behavior. The typical eye exam still involves the use of some form of the classic Snellen eye chart — the well-known stationary, high-contrast letters in a darkened room. Dutch ophthalmologist, Herman Snellen, developed this chart in 1862, long before people were scrolling on mobile phone and computer screens. No one had experienced traffic stimulating peripheral eyesight or movies that featured many special effects that simultaneously activated eyes and ears.

What science tells us now is that we should also test awareness of visual surroundings. What we see —whether consciously or subconsciously — changes behavior. This is especially true in academic settings. In a classroom, there is constant eye movement as a student's gaze shifts from book to teacher to board to desk, etc., while simultaneously listening to what the teacher is saying and filtering out other sounds and sights. If a child has hypersensitive peripheral systems, he can be distracted by ambient noise in his ears, or movement processed out of the "corner" of his eyes.

The eye is comprised of brain tissue and contains astounding and intricate filtering systems. For example, the optic nerve provides exiting and entering signals, which connect to the body at a reflex level through both voluntary and involuntary systems. Other, slower signals traveling in the optic nerve include those for external awareness of space and internal perception. Many signals are considered non-image forming, and aren't used for eyesight.

As part of the brain, the eye interacts with many systems and can tune out external noise, or become hypersensitive to it. We have the capacity today to orchestrate body systems through stimulation of the retina. This is possible because peripheral retinal connections impact brain function. The eyes can also indicate systemic problems. The following examples are well documented (see listed references):

- Eye-movement function (or dysfunction, as the case may be) can predict post-concussion syndrome.
- Large pupil size is an indication of an overloaded fight or flight nervous system.
- Vascular changes can be measured through retinal evaluation, neurological fluctuations can be determined by optic nerve changes.
- Endocrine systems assessed from sugar levels in tears.
- Liver function can be measured indirectly by evaluation of the sclera.
- Sleep patterns also can be evaluated through the eye.
- Posture changes in the neck, back or hips can affect eye movements.

If a child has protective reflexes hindering his or her eye movement ranges, external awareness of surroundings will be limited. While watching a teacher moving around, a child with a limited eye movement range will be forced to use upper and lower body movements to compensate. The resulting fidgeting (shifting weight in the classroom seat) will pull the child's attention away from the teacher.

Our many visual pathways work together like an orchestra. Each delicately balanced system remains within a "comfort zone," due to the multitude of behind-the-scenes processes. A common belief is that the process of seeing is simply an input function; namely, light enters the eye and, the brain registers that information and "sees" what the objects are. In truth, seeing is much more comprehensive — and complicated. The many visual systems synchronize external inputs from other senses with internal processing of the mind and body.

A neuro-optometrist can determine if a person is operating outside their "comfort zone" or within their "tolerance zone." A child in a comfort zone can deal with whatever comes, including watching or listening to a teacher. The external "orchestra" sections include object perception (targets) and spatial awareness (background). The background sets the stage for aiming accurately and focusing clearly on the selected target. The internal "orchestra" sections involve processing a mixture of signal inputs beneath a conscious level, such as breathing and posture.

Another example which includes subconscious balancing of comfort and tolerance ranges is running. Internal and external processes of the mind and the body are separate, yet interconnected. When running for fun, the brain often zones out, and the body runs on autopilot at a speed within the comfort range.

However, when a person is running because he or she is late for a bus, thoughts of being late can cause stress and put the person in tolerance mode, running a bit faster than is comfortable. Understandably, running away from life-threatening situation will put the person into a protective mode, and leads to a complete sensory overload and a much longer recovery. Eye movement is similar. A child who needs to use a tolerance mode to maintain eye control during reading will have more trouble comprehending. The executive functions in the mind take a back seat to survival functions in the body.

Awareness and attention are also affected by the internal senses. If a child has a headache, a stomach ache or a runny nose, peripheral awareness is tuned out, and attention on the teacher may be hindered. When only focusing on one detail, and not using eyes and ears as a team, a child often misses the big picture.

Observed behaviors — what we can see children doing — are the outward manifestations of internal processing. Sensory inputs from the surroundings combine with body signals and internal perception. The combination contributes to awareness and attention, which in turn stimulate aiming and focusing, leading to conscious eyesight.

Behavior then, is an output that follows the extensive filtering of both internal and external sensory information. Because of the integration of these many processes, effectively addressing a child's behavioral or learning disorders or other system breakdowns, requires coordination across a variety of testing modes and treatment models.

There are four main types of eye care professionals who evaluate people with learning problems. Optometrists and ophthalmologists emphasize function and structure, respectively. Neuro-ophthalmologists use the known pathways between the body and the eye to diagnose disease, and neuro-optometrists induce body changes through the eye.

In summary, it is hoped that learning and behavioral problems can be assessed from a non-traditional perspective, by evaluating systems in a team rather than individually. A child who is disruptive in class might have a lack of synchronization between visual and auditory systems. If so, eyeglasses designed to coordinate those mismatched sensory signals can help the child watch and listen to a teacher in a classroom.

The visual system is a critical system to assess thoroughly (considering that over 1.2 million brain signals arise from each eye as opposed to only 30,000 from each ear). But is only one of many facets to evaluate. The process of seeing is a complicated one, and a deeper understanding of the mechanisms contributing to visual processing will help scientists comprehend individual perception, cognition and behavior.

Collaboration and coordination among professionals is vital for the maximal benefit of patients, given our increased knowledge of how the mind and body are interconnected.

"If you pull the camera back on life, and it doesn't change your perspective, pull it back farther!"

--KATHE MAZUR

EMPOWERING PARENTS AND EDUCATORS

This book and the opinions expressed are in no way trying to replace the clinical advice of your eye care professional. It is an opportunity to empower you as parents or teachers to enable you to ask the right questions. If your routine eye care professional does not have a practice focussed on visual skills and visual processing, and you have a child that struggles academically, ask them to direct you to one that does.

Below is a simple 5-point checklist for parents to present to their eye doctor when asking whether their child has intact and functioning visual skills. Be aware; this list has some extra tests that are considered over and above a routine eye examination. However, if the patient fails either the CITT questionnaire or the COVD Quality of Life Questionnaire below or has an IEP in place in school for spelling, reading and for written output, then regardless of the test examination results, the child will likely require a more in-depth assessment.

CITT Questionnaire (0-60 score, >15 considered a fail)

Tick the appropriate box and then total each column and use weighting multiplier at bottom to get final score

Question to Ask Patient (Parent if child under 12)	Never	Not often	Sometimes	Fairly often	Always
1 - Do your eyes feel tired when reading or doing close work?	☐	☐	☐	☐	☐
2 - Do your eyes feel uncomfortable when reading?	☐	☐	☐	☐	☐
3 - Do you have headaches when reading?	☐	☐	☐	☐	☐
4 - Do you feel sleepy when reading?	☐	☐	☐	☐	☐
5 - Do you lose concentration when reading?	☐	☐	☐	☐	☐
6 - Do you have trouble remembering what you have read?	☐	☐	☐	☐	☐
7 - Do you have double vision when reading?	☐	☐	☐	☐	☐
8 - Do you see the words move or jump when you read?	☐	☐	☐	☐	☐
9 - Do you feel like you read slowly?	☐	☐	☐	☐	☐
10 - Do your eyes ever hurt when reading?	☐	☐	☐	☐	☐
11 - Do your eyes ever feel sore (i.e. achy) when reading?	☐	☐	☐	☐	☐
12 - Do you ever feel a "pulling feeling" around your eyes?	☐	☐	☐	☐	☐
13 - Do you notice words coming in and out of focus?	☐	☐	☐	☐	☐
14 - Do you lose your place / line when reading?	☐	☐	☐	☐	☐
15 - Do you have to re-read the same line when reading?	☐	☐	☐	☐	☐
Multiply total score in column by FACTOR Add scores in the boxes to the right (score of > 15 a fail)	x 0	x 1	x 2	x 3	x 4

CITT Questionnaire
Scale 0-60
Score of >15 some concern
>20 significant concern
Can be used on ages 6-18 years old

Quality of Life Checklist

Patient Name: _____

Form Completed by: _____

Date: _____

Check the column which best represents the occurrence of each symptom	Never 0	Seldom 1	Occasionally 2	Frequently 3	Always 4
Blurred close vision					
Double vision					
Headaches with near work					
Words run together reading					
Burning, itchy, watery eyes					
Falls asleep reading					
Sees worse at the end of day					
Skips/repeats lines reading					
Dizzy/nauseated by near work					
Head tilt/one eye closed to read					
Difficulty copying from chalkboard					
Avoids near work/reading					
Omits small words when reading					
Writes uphill/downhill					
Misaligns digits/columns of numbers					
Poor reading comprehension					
Poor/inconsistent in sports					
Holds reading too close					
Trouble keeping attention on reading					
Difficulty completing work on time					
Says "I can't" before trying					
Avoids sports/games					
Poor hand/eye coordination					
Poor handwriting					
Does not judge distance accurately					
Clumsy, knocks things over					
Poor time use/management					
Does not make change well					
Loses things/belongings					
Car or motion sickness					
Forgetfulness/poor memory					
Total for each column:	_ x 0 = 0	_ x1 = _	_ x2 = _	_ x3 = _	_ x4 = _

Grand Total: _____

<15 = Routine eye exam recommended

16-24 = Comprehensive exam with developmental OD recommended

>25 = Developmental vision problem likely, comprehensive exam with developmental OD strongly recommended

215 W. Garfield Rd, Suite 200 Aurora, OH 44202 | 330-995-0718 | www.covd.org

Start the conversation with your eye care professional.

Ask your regular doctor for a 0-10 score in each section below, with 0 being impaired and ten being perfectly intact. Some of these tests are routine tests, and some are from the more in-depth test list, however, especially if your child has an IEP or reading based issues at school, then these five critical tests need to be done and quantified in some way. Any area with a score of less than 6 is a problem.

Highest Yield Clinical Test Checklist:

GENERAL TERM	SCORE (0-10)	POSSIBLE TESTS TO QUANTIFY	NORM
Tracking skills testing	**DOCTOR TO INSERT RESULT**	DEM test, King Devick testing	>50th percentile
Convergence testing	**DOCTOR TO INSERT RESULT**	NPC Test, Prism bar testing in free space	<8cm (3 times repeatedly) from the nose. Break point at least 20PD, recovery at least 16PD
Near point focusing ability	**DOCTOR TO INSERT RESULT**	MAF, BAF, Monocular Amplitudes of Accommodation (DS)	+/- 2DS, ideally >10cpm) Use 18-5 - 1/3 of age as expected value for amplitudes of accommodation.
Hyperopia (Long-sightedness)	**DOCTOR TO INSERT RESULT**	Cycloplegia (drops) with result	At or above +1.25DS flagged
Vergence Facility Test	**DOCTOR TO INSERT RESULT**	12BO/3BI at near testing	Normal at least 15 cpm at near

> All 5 test are crucial if IEP in place.
> Any 1 area flagged warrants a more in-depth assessment/referral

There is a wonderful group called "Vision Therapy Parents Unite" led by a wonderful person, Michele Hillman. I have met Michele and she is nothing short of a saint in my mind. She created a very powerful group on Facebook which now numbers over 20,000 members. These members are parents of children with vision-based learning difficulties who have gone through or are currently going through the process of Optometric Vision Therapy. https://www.facebook.com/groups/VTparentsunite

It is a fantastic forum for parents to connect with other parents on their experiences and a great place to ask questions. VTPU also has many resources available to members of the group from research papers to forms and advice from other parents who have gone through the process.

Michele received an award from COVD International in 2015 called the "Making Vision Therapy Visible Award." This is even more special in that very few non-doctors have received this award. Michelle has single-handedly resulted I am sure in literally thousands of parents being able to better navigate the system and find out true facts about vision therapy. Michele, I would like to personally in this book say a massive "Thank you" for all you have done for Optometric Vision Therapy and children in need around the world. You are a superstar! If you have any questions that you would like to ask other parents on this topic who have dealt with the process - I recommend this great resource! Read more about Michele's story. https://tinyurl.com/quaid-asd-story

"At the end of the day, the most overwhelming key to a child's success is the positive involvement of parents."

JANE D HULL

CELEBRATING THE TEACHERS

This chapter is a dedication to educators. Let me begin by paying homage to the gargantuan efforts that educators give in classrooms across the world. I can name three educators who have made a massive difference in my life by small, passing comments they made to me. These comments made a world of difference in motivating me to keep pushing despite my own difficulties with both speech and visual issues.

Teachers are often under-appreciated and under-supported. Let me paint a picture for you of the stress and unfair pressure teachers are placed under within an educational system. They are often faced with large class sizes, ranging from 25-35 students at a time. In 2013, 1 in 10 students required an Individualized Educational Plan (IEP). The pressure is mounting on teachers to improve those results. This is closer to 2 in 10 today.

One question continues to loom – who is providing educators with the resources and tools to make this enhanced level of education a reality? Who is helping them answer why the rates of IEPs continue to increase within our school system? Why is a large portion of these children continuing to struggle? Is it fair to hold teachers responsible for the results the children can attain without giving educators all the important tools to achieve this task?

There was a time when some educators associated lack of concentration as defiance. Many years ago, my father, Eamon Quaid did not get his first pair of glasses until he was 12 years old. Over his early years, he struggled to read. He remembers a teacher pushing his head closer to the page to get him to concentrate on his reading. Only after he was tested did they learn that he needed a +6 prescription for glasses. Those are the glasses with extremely thick lenses. Pushing him closer to the book was exactly the opposite of what he needed. Studies have shown that hyperopia as low as +2 DS (dioptres) can trigger enough symptoms on the Connors Rating Scale (CRS) to incorrectly indicate an ADHD diagnosis.

Thankfully, teachers and other educators nowadays understand so much more about the connection between seeing and learning. The information in this book will add another layer of understanding to the important work that educators do. My dad would have thrived in school had he been a child today with educators who had an awareness of visual processing in their toolbox.

In a later chapter, you will read about the complete process of developing an IEP. Before a student is put onto a formal IEP, a detailed Psycho-Educational Assessment is conducted, usually by the Board of Education's psychologist. These tests can have great value. A "Psych-Ed" assessment has a large visual component to it. Our research has shown that every child with an IEP should have an in-depth assessment of the oculomotor and visual processing system rather than a routine eye exam. This is for one simple reason. The child can be helped. This is powerful information.

When a child fails to thrive in reading and/or writing, and all standard assessments are "normal," something important is missing. We should not be content with a vague label like ADHD or dyslexia that fits the child into a box.

We as healthcare professionals need to enable and equip educators with the latest data. That way, they have yet another tool to help them guide parents to "looking under every rock." This will ensure that all children reach their maximum potential. Then, all students will have the opportunity to access the curriculum in a fair and equitable manner.

Many children we encounter are diagnosed with NVLD, or Non-Verbal Learning Disorder. This means that the child is at or often above grade level when speaking or listening. However, when reading or writing, which requires vision, they are often severely below grade level. This child may in fact not have a learning disability but an un-treated and undiagnosed visual-skills issue. We would be remiss in jumping to a diagnosis before all other routes have been explored with proper remediation of any diagnosed visual issues occurring first.

As a parent, I understand that an educator is not a healthcare pro-fessional. They are, however, trained and experienced in identifying behavioral traits in children that may suggest underlying issues that will interfere with learning. If your child's educator suggests that you, as a parent, have their child's vision assessed; they are only *making an observation in the best interests of the child.* It is up to the parent to take the advice and follow through. The healthcare professional is then given the opportunity to diagnose any issue properly. The teacher should be applauded for noticing and caring about their student's success. They are making a huge difference as they work together with the parents as partners in education.

We have had many children recommended to our clinics based on the sage advice of a teacher **who cared.** It does make a difference in helping a child succeed. In these cases, we usually witnessed two key factors. A parent cared enough to listen. A teacher was brave enough to bring up the issue with a parent, even though it may have resulted in an uncomfortable conversation.

In Ontario, we often only see action at grade 3 and grade 6 because of poor results on the standardized EQAO scores. These standardized tests measure the core areas of reading, writing, and mathematics. If a child scores very poorly, alarm bells ring. Teachers, however, often see the issues brewing much earlier. Accommodations may be put in place if the child cannot read. The child may be given a laptop that reads to them or uses voice to text. These again are accommodations. They are not really solutions. These children need help, and the sooner this occurs, the better.

Waiting to see if benchmark results improve by waiting for the child to mature is often chosen. If an underlying functional issue that can be treated is the problem, valuable time can be wasted, and the child forms a greater dislike of the education experience over time.

There is testing available to spot those children heading for academic issues as early as senior kindergarten to first grade in the form of a visual skills assessment (i.e., both oculomotor and visual skills assessments.) Now imagine if we could put a percentile on every visual skill, motor-based, and visual processing to match what is age-appropriate for a child. What if you could rank them? What a powerful tool that would be! This would allow the educational system a chance to get ahead of these issues and be proactive, rather than reactive. This invaluable tool is available via a VSA assessment.

I will never fault a teacher for advising an assessment; even if it turns out that the student is fine. It will be helpful to add to the educator's toolbox the recommendation for a VSA assessment. This is especially helpful when their student is struggling on a daily basis with reading and or writing. The evidence in the literature is too great now to ignore the link between reading issues and visual skills deficiencies. It is so strong that I believe that the awareness of the importance of visual skills should be included as part of teacher college training. Let me encourage all educators who have students with any of these issues to reach out to an optometry professional, specifically, if possible, someone certified by the College of Optometrists in Vision Development (COVD) with an FCOVD accreditation. (See www.covd. org for more information.) When as an educator, you believe there is a barrier to learning present, be brave in speaking to the parents of that child. Recommend that they have their child's visual skills addressed thoroughly if there is an IEP in place or suspected to be required. Parents, continue to encourage open dialogue with your child's teacher. I sometimes gain great insights into how a child functions from speaking with their teacher. We all need to play our part.

Teachers represent a positive influence on society. They can affect powerful change in a child's life. Be open with parents of the children who appear to struggle under your watch. Ensure that students have a proper and thorough workup of their visual system. Ensure that a proper hearing assessment is done. Are there any speech issues to be addressed? That referral may be the pivotal event in that child's life that puts them back on the road to educational success and ultimately allows them equitable access to the curriculum.

"Everyone who remembers his own education remembers teachers, not methods and techniques. The teacher is the heart of the educational system."

SIDNEY HOOK

WHAT IS OPTOMETRIC VISION THERAPY?

To understand the *process* of Vision Therapy (VT), let me take you through the typical flow of procedures. If the brain has lost its ability to team the eyes together, VT (also known as Neuro-Optometric Visual Rehabilitation) is required. When an image from our dynamic world falls on the retina of each eye, the brain must visually reconstruct the information in a way that is useful and integrates with other senses. The ultimate goal of visual perception is to make sense of the world around us, and ultimately, to allow us to move effectively in the visual space around us. How each eye's image is coordinated to create what we "see" ultimately occurs in the brain, not in the eye itself. This is a key concept to understand about VT.

Before we start therapy, we need to measure several standardized oculomotor metrics and standardized visual processing metrics with normative data. (i.e., what is typical for these values in the general population without visual issues?) These metrics are listed in Table 1 below in the form of a sample progress report. If more information is required on the details of the techniques, there is an excellent medical book called, "Applied Concepts in Vision Therapy," by Dr. Leonard Press, OD FCOVD.

OCULOMOTOR DATA (*remains a concern)

Testing	Baseline- August 1/17	Current	Goal (at least)
Symptom score CITT Study	34/60	20/60*	<15/60
Accommodative Facility OD (+/-2DS)	2cpm (issue with -)	8cpm	12cpm
Accommodative Facility OS (+/-2DS)	3cpm (issues with -)	8cpm	12cpm
Stereo (Depth Perception)	140" (3/10)	60" (8/10)	40" (10/10) with global
Vergence Facility (12BO/3BI at 40cm)	6cpm	10cpm	15cpm
Visual Acuity OD	20/50	20/20	20/20
Visual Acuity OS	20/40	20/20	20/20
Near Point of Convergence (NPC)	25cm	10cm	<7cm
Vergence Amplitude (positive at near)	-/8/6	-/20/18	-/25/20

VISUAL PROCESSING (percentiles, * still concern)

Testing (DTVP-A)	Baseline	Current	Goal (at least)
Copying	5th	60th	37th-50th
Figure Ground	50th	91st	37th-50th
Vis- Motor Search	9th	*15th	37th-50th
Visual Closure	50th	63rd	37th-50th
Vis- Motor Speed	50th	63rd	37th-50th
Form Constancy	25th	91st	37th-50th
Visual Memory	8th	37rd	37th-50th
DEM. Vertical tracking / saccades	1st	35th	37th-50th
DEM. Horizontal tracking / saccades	<1st	20th	37th-50th
TOSWRF-2 reading efficiency	5th	50th	37th-50th

Percentile guide
<25th= impaired, 25th - 36th = mildly impaired, 37th - 50th = low average, ≥50th = normal

It is the brain's task to process the meaning of the images that fall on each retina. The brain must take the two sets of information streaming in from both eyes, process them together, and recreate the image in a meaningful way. If the brain is injured in some way, it will not be able to team the eyes as it should and then weave that information together as easily, resulting in any number of issues.

The main aim of Vision Therapy is to awaken the brain in regaining or acquiring the correct way to process visual information via proper control of several eye-teaming skills. Sometimes, we have to break down "bad adaptations" to rebuild the foundation of proper visual perception. After all, remember Hebb's Law; "Nerves that fire together wire together?" This law can also work to our detriment. Our visual processing pathways are like highways of visual information. They can also weave together inappropriately. In that case, the brain would develop an adaptation to avoid problems like double vision. However, the cost of this adaptation is a loss of the visual functionality and flexibility required to handle various visual challenges.

In pediatric cases, if a patient's eyes are pointing in different directions, the child sees two of everything. It does not take long for the brain to actively inhibit seeing one of the images. In the VT world, we call this "suppression." Just as the brain can suppress bad memories, the brain can also suppress inconsistent and confusing visual information so it can make some sense of the world. The visual system will almost always choose suppression over double vision. This makes sense from a survival standpoint. If every threat you saw in the wilderness looked like two dangers, you would have a 50/50 chance of choosing the correct one from which to flee. You would not survive long.

Suppression then is one of the more pronounced maladaptations or dysfunctions that need to be reversed with Vision Therapy. There are many, far more subtle, maladaptations that also arise. One of the least discussed challenges is the loss of tracking abilities. This ultimately can lead to the loss of visual memory (accurately recalling visually what you have seen.) When the eyes receive different information, the brain gets conflicting signals. This is a problem. Any disruption in the visual processing pathways will result in an extra load on the other sensory systems. Tracking issues occur then because the brain tries to reduce the amount of conflicting visual information is has to process. This results in what is known as "collapsed peripheral awareness", or put more simply, the brain reduced processing of the areas around what we are looking at in order to reduce the mis-match.

The term PA refers to the brain not just processing WHAT it is looking at, but also perceiving WHERE it is looking, relative to every-thing around it. When the eyes do not align appropriately, not only is the "WHAT" you are looking at misaligned, but more importantly, all the areas around what you are looking at are also misaligned. This will be different for each eye. To cope with the massive peripheral visual mismatch it is seeing, the brain's visual system has to adapt. Usually, it has to reduce the PA system of at least one eye (sometimes both) in order to reduce the overall visual confusion. This maladaptation is required, but if not addressed, it will adversely affect other sensory systems, such as Executive Function (i.e., Can I remember what I read because my eyes are jumping around too much on the page.)

Here is an example to demonstrate PA. First, write your name in cursive, they way you normally would. Now, write it again but this time with a key difference, *look at the pen tip 100% of the time.* You will find it very different, challenging, and much more tiring. The simple explanation is that you did not use PA the second time. You were not using your peripheral visual system to give you a better overall vis-ual-spatial perspective but instead were hyper-focused on the pen tip.

A good analogy here would be to imagine you are driving a car. Initially, the car has power steering and driving is a breeze. You switch on the radio, and you even have a chat with your friend sitting beside you in the passenger seat. Now, imagine that all of a sudden, the power steering starts to fail and act strangely. You now must work to control the car, although you still *can* control it. You find that the first thing you do is to turn off the radio and stop talking to your friend. You do these things because now you have to put more energy into concen-trating on controlling the car.

This is what happens when the eyes of a child no longer correctly teaming together. If they are in a classroom and have to copy from the board to their page while simultaneously trying to listen to the teacher who is speaking, it is a problem. The child only has the energy to concentrate on the one thing; and even that is difficult and tiring, due to their visual issues.

When a child is referred to us for an assessment, comments about low working memory or executive function are consistently mentioned in reports. When a visual skills issue is identified, it is likely more accurate to state that their Executive Function/Working Memory or their "attention" was being taxed by the extra effort required to function visually. The solution then with children exhibiting these symptoms is to deal with the underlying visual issues first, in the hopes that the 40% of the brain's visual machinery starts to work more efficiently. Research at the National Institute of Health (NIH) level is showing that VT helps academics overall. Rather than accept the adaptation or give it a name, we should be dealing with the dysfunction itself to resolve it. This is the reason for Vision Therapy.

There may, of course, be other issues other than vision to consider when a child is struggling in school. There is always a bigger picture. However, the largest sensory system in the brain should not be ignored. Even if there are other issues at play, every child deserves to have a visual system that works as efficiently as possible given this system's sensory dominance.

With all the general medical groundwork laid, let us look at the flow of steps taken in the process of Vision Therapy. In our clinics, we usually work with the patient for one hour per week. A session generally consists of 45mins of active therapy and then 15 minutes of counselling patients on in-home VT exercises that re-enforce gains made at our clinic. This homework is vital to continuing the progress achieved in the clinic. The VT sessions in the office are there to teach the techniques. The home VT sessions are there to perfect the techniques. We rescore all VT oculomotor and visual processing skills every 12 in-office sessions to ensure improvements are actually occurring. These progress evaluations or PEs are critical.

Family support and encouragement are so important in this process. As the patient undergoes the therapy, the parents have to support the child's endeavors and help them with the home VT. The child in VT needs constant positive re-enforcement, even if they struggle with a technique. When they succeed, genuine praise is critical, especially if one considers they are used to "Just struggling." It is important to remind them that their *visual system needs help*! VT allows your visual system to become more flexible so that you can handle any visual challenge in life.

"Intelligence is the ability to adapt to change. It is not the strongest of the species that survives, but the one that is best able to adapt to change."

CHARLES DARWIN

WELCOME TO OUR CLINIC

It is the first consultation at our clinic. We often ask our pediatric patients who range from 5-19 years old and who have reading difficulties, a series of conversationally toned questions.

First of all, I always make a point of raising the child to the doctor's chair level, so they are eye-to-eye with me when I am speaking to them. By putting the child at eye level, you are saying to the child, "I am listening to you, and mainly you right now, and you deserve to be heard."

After chatting and putting the child at ease, the child usually beams because they are now the center of attention and they feel free to say whatever they want. It is a very empowering statement to a child and in fact, often encourages them to open up and try to describe what is happening to them. This is very liberating and cathartic for some kids! Trust me on this – I personally lived this as a child, often peering up to a towering doctor which would resulting in me saying literally nothing.

I often ask simple questions about whether they "see two of things" or "if words drift in and out of being clear sometimes?" I remain neutral in my tone as I do not wish to lead the child either way. On the other hand, I also want them to feel comfortable in terms of describing how they see. I am constantly amazed how many kids affirm that they are seeing "two of things" and then with their hands proceed to show me exactly how they see two things at the same time. Often they just say "Yeah, things go fuzzy and funny at near all the time." Parents are often shocked and say something to their child along the lines of, "Why didn't you tell me?" Some kids often respond with something along the lines of, "Well, you didn't ask." More commonly, the child responds by saying, "But I always see that way." We then have to remind ourselves that if someone has always seen a certain way, to him or her, that is normal. We have to remember this crucial point as parents and doctors! Like those with a color deficiency, if no one ever told the person that they were not seeing all the colors, they would likely live their life oblivious to the fact that they had a problem. Of course, in color vision issues, there is no significant functional issue other than color discrimination. In oculomotor issues and visual processing issues, the problems can cause operational issues - a nightmare for a child trying to cope within a classroom environment.

We often joke with the patients in our clinic that all the doctors in our practice wished we had a screen that we could attach to our patient's heads to allow us to see the world exactly as they do. Maybe one day, that will be possible. For now, we need both objective and subjective clinical tools when making visual diagnoses.

Subjective tools that mainly rely on the responses of the patient or parent alone can be misleading. Fortunately, we have both subjective and objective tools in the eye care arena, and when used properly, they can be powerfully effective. One objective test we use is observing how the child's eyes move when moving inwards towards the nose (converging). This skill is required for all near tasks, including reading. Take a pen and ask a child to follow it towards their nose. This can often show very quickly that one or both of the eyes are unable to team together. When reading, we should be able to comfortably move the eyes inwards, to within about 3 inches (8 cm) from the bridge of our nose. This is one of some fifteen different objective tests we can do. A similar number of subjective tests for visual processing ability is available. Each child then is given a percentile (i.e., 50th percentile average, 5th percentile very low, etc.). This can be thought of as quantifying the "hardware" and "software" of the visual system.

As a parent with a child who struggles to remember what words look like (and how to recall spelling visually not phonetically), you want to know what the status of your visual hardware and software is.

Welcome to our clinic. This is what we aim to do – inform and provide strategies to improve visual skills.

We look with our eyes. However, our brain processes what we see and what it means based on prior experience. That is the key. Think of the lens on your smartphone. If we take a picture, the image is just raw data. It is meaningless until it is interpreted. To see the image it has to be processed using the software in your phone that turns the data into an image on your screen. Our brain takes the image our eyes pass along over the optic nerve and processes it. Not only does it give us an image to see, but it also provides a three-dimensional analysis, context, memory, and so much more – all in an instant. You begin to appreciate the complexity of our brain's immense processing power.

What is the big idea to catch here?

We don't see with our eyes, we see with our brain.

The eyes send the signal, but the brain is where the complex processing takes place. After all, why else did nature give us two eyes if not to see the world from two slightly different angles? This allows us to appreciate the visual advantage of depth perception.

This gift is a double-edged sword because when issues do arise with the hardware, the brain's inability to control the eyes will result in problems with visual processing. It is important to understand that the physical eye is healthy (i.e. retina etc.), but the function is what is impaired. With this symbiotic relationship, however, any condition that affects the brain will also affect how the eyes team together. It is a two-way street. Examples causing disruption to the brain can include concussion. It can also result from any developmental issue that affects brain development. This includes prematurity. Of note, any child greater than 3 weeks premature or less than 5lbs 5oz birth weight has been shown to be higher risk for eye misalignment issues. Once again, this illustrates the fallacy of the "eye exam" statement, in that the term implies that we are only examining the eyes. Our diagnostic tests examine how the eyes, the brain, and the body are communicating together.

Exploring how we see is not as simple as asking, "Can you read the letters on the chart?" The more thorough approaches ask more in-depth questions, such as, "Can you see a 3D image quickly and without making you feel sick?" "Can you remember the sequence of symbols you just saw and reproduce them?" "How many eye movements does it take you to read 100 words and how much of what you read can you recall?" Eyesight and vision are very different things. Eyesight is "20/20" but vision is how efficiently and accurately you process what you see. You can have good eyesight but terrible vision, depending on how your brain interprets what you are seeing. By only ever looking at eyesight, you never really get to understand how a person really "sees."

It is also worth noting that without good visual skills, an individ-ual will also likely have poor insight (i.e., the ability to be simply aware of how they interact with others and also how to critique the external world appropriately.) After all, at least 40% of the brain is primarily visual machinery.

Do they:

- Understand what they see
- Retain what they see
- Be able to reproduce and give their thoughts on what they have seen
- Be able to have insight on observation

This point is where we need to understand both the hardware and the software of the visual system. Seeing "20/20" can still mean that there are issues with all of the above points, if visual skills are deficient.

After all, a computer can look fine structurally but still not work if the underlying code or software is a mess. For those of you who are computer-savvy, we can also bring in the analogy of RAM (Rapid Access Memory). RAM is what allows a computer to run fast. The more RAM, the faster the computer will run programs, but this is as-suming that the RAM is not being used for something else other than the speed of processing. What is the first thing that happens to the speed of your computer if there is a hardware or software problem? It slows down. Ok, so is the RAM the issue? Of course it is not. There are software and/or hardware issues causing the computer issue. This illustration is a good analogy for visual function and what can happen to the "attention ability" of a child overall. The attention ability of the child is like the RAM. If there is a hardware or software issue, the RAM is affected, and the attention ability of the child decreases.

Now, will treating oculomotor (visual hardware) and visual processing (visual software) issues improve attention and reading ability? In our experience, the answer is usually yes. However, to be clear, we are *eye doctors,* and we treat the visual system. The issue, however, is that we distinguish vision rather than eyesight. Vision permeates a massive proportion of the human brain. Eyesight is just an eye chart, which when used in isolation, is not of much use. Surprising as that sounds, you can have a great reader who sees 20/20 and a terrible reader who sees 20/20. So the eye chart by itself is useless in predicting how a child reads. It is important to define what we mean by *vision.*

However, reading is highly predictable when one looks at all 17 or so visual skills involved in vision as a whole. Vision is the "big picture" whereas eyesight is just one cog in a complex process.

Just consider an anatomical fact for a moment. Each eye has an optic nerve at the back of it. This is the part of the eye that projects connections to the brain. To be precise, the optic nerve is *actually brain tissue.* Each optic nerve has about 1.2 million ganglion cells (think of them as wires) connecting to the rest of the brain. Between the two eyes, we have 2.4 million ganglion cells. These ganglion cells come from approximately 127 million rods and cones per retina. Keep those numbers in mind for a moment. Now let us look at the auditory (hearing) system, which has a total of about 30,000 ganglion cells per ear, or 60,000 ganglion cells in total. Vision is indeed a very dominant sense anatomically.

I am not for a second saying that hearing is not necessary - quite the contrary, I am highlighting how much neural machinery in the brain is dedicated to vision. When it comes to children with reading issues, we especially need to appreciate the dominance of the visual system and look at it in much more detail than merely "20/20" on a chart, at 20 feet away. After all, reading is not a natural task. There is nothing in nature that mimics reading. We hardly ever cross our eyes towards our nose for an extended period of time. Yet, we ask our eyes that are turned inwards to move from side to side while also looking at small symbols to infer meaning. This task is always a challenge for even a perfectly intact visual system. Imagine if your eyes struggled!

The brain pays so much attention to vision it gravitates toward it when the other senses are ambiguous. I show parents something called the "McGurk Effect." (I encourage you to look it up online and watch a video about it. My Ph.D. was in visual illusions. You are correct if you think that sounds way better than psychophysics!) This particular illusion never ceases to fascinate me. In a nutshell, the McGurk effect shows someone stating the word "BAA BAA BAA" over, and over and the mouth movements match the "B" sound. The fascinating part is that if the mouth movements now are made to look like the person is saying "FAA FAA FAA" but the sound is not changed, you hear what the mouth movements *imply*. When you turn your back to the image, you hear it as the sound indeed is (i.e., BAA BAA BAA). It is a fantastic illusion to watch. The illusion shows how the mouth movements we see can actively influence what we believe we are hearing. What we see can easily over-ride what we hear. This fact comes as no shock to me as an eye doctor, given the anatomical discussion earlier (i.e., 2.4m neurones for the eyes versus 60,000 neurones for the ears) but it is amazing how little attention we give to vision as a sensory system in learning difficulties.

Illusions often give us a unique insight into how the visual system can help or hinder us. In seeing many of these cases in the past, I am convinced of one simple truth. The visual system is either helping or hindering. It is rarely in between. Given the high amount of neural machinery dedicated to visual processing, it is evident to me as a clinician and researcher that the visual system needs to be understood in greater detail in learning difficulty cases. The exciting thing is that we are just likely scratching the surface!

"Smart people learn from everything and everyone, average people from their experiences, stupid people have all the answers."

SOCRATES

HOPE FOR PARENTS

Our children are by far our most precious assets. In addition to being an eye doctor, I am also a parent. Looking at my child, and from my experience growing up, I strongly empathize with parents where there are paediatric learning difficulties. It can be nothing short of devastating to be told that your child has a problem.

My mother once said to me that I would never know true selflessness until I had my own child. Of course, I did not really understand what she meant until I did have a child of my own. Now, of course, I get that and fully appreciate that comment!

We will do anything for our children. They are helpless and entirely dependent on us in their early life. We view them as an extension of ourselves. True love invests something of us into that other human being. Their ability to succeed in whatever their potential is within the educational system is a vital part of this process. This is why a learning challenge diagnosis is usually scary for parents. It destroys the expectation of a future full of hope and promise expected to be handed down from parent to child.

I hope to give encouragement to parents in this situation and reduce the false guilt many of them feel when faced with uncertain futures for their children. Parents often worry, "Am I doing enough?" "Did I miss something?" "Was this my fault?" I have heard a lot of these sentiments from parents in my clinic consultations over the years. It amazes me that despite these parents being heroes in championing support for their children, they continue to blame themselves. I think this all goes back to our DNA to see your child to thrive and succeed.

There is always a balance to be struck in paediatric learning difficulty cases. On one side, if there is a TRUE developmental delay or diagnosis (i.e., ASD, Asperger's, Connective Tissue Disorders etc.), these conditions must be taken into account. They are real and must be acknowledged as important factors. They may make the prognosis more guarded. However, we cannot and must not define the patient by their condition.

In our clinic, we never use the phrase, "an autistic child." Instead, that patient is referred to as "a child with autism." There is a unique person behind the diagnosis; there is no one else on the planet like them. They are unique, and this must also be acknowledged. A patient with autism deserves to have their visual issues addressed - just as much as a person without autism.

This philosophy has always been my guiding principle. Inform the parents of the findings and have an open and honest conversation with them about the process of rehabilitation. The prognosis must be tempered by the over-arching conditions present. It is exciting to have treated numerous patients with concurrent conditions, who impressed me with their progress.

My conversations usually center on MRP or Maximum Rehabilitative Potential. We need to be honest. We ultimately don't know what a child's MRP is until we begin treating them. This is especially true for children on an IEP who have a learning issue but have no obvious developmental delay or other diagnoses. The parents, along the way, would have been informed of their child's struggle to read and write in school. From a vision perspective or from other types of interventions such as Speech and Language Pathology, Audiological Processing, or Occupational Therapy, we have to allow every child the opportunity to receive appropriate therapy. That includes a therapy done in the right sequence to ensure that they reach their MRP.

The other side of this conversation is to understand when to stop. The danger is that since this is such an important area to the parents of these children, therapy may continue without having any clear indication of whether or not it is helping. The key here is progress evaluations. I tell all the parents in our clinic that we are accountable to them, on a periodic basis, to prove whether the intervention is helping or not. Using processing metrics and oculomotor data, we can show parents that the therapy is helping.

We have a general flow where we tend to start with the body (i.e., retained primitive reflexes, OT work) and then move towards vision, and visual decoding. From there, we move to hearing/phonological encoding, using testing to determine whether it is likely one or the other. The phrase, "Proper diagnosis before giving a prognosis." is a guiding principle of our clinic.

In summary, parents, you are the hero in the life of your child. You are the ones that continually advocate getting the best for your child. We, as healthcare professionals, need to ensure that we are giving the right recommendations, to the right people, at the right time. You must never feel guilt or shame. You should not feel responsible for the learning issues your child is experiencing. You should however continue to inform yourself, as to the correct approach and sequence of interventions that will help your child.

"The child is the beauty of God in the world."

MOTHER THERESA

GAMES

Are there simple things that can be done to determine if a child requires further intervention?

Five Vision Games you can play at home or in the classroom to subtly screen your child for possible vision issues are listed below. The focus of these games is to assess where your child's vision might be at and not to treat the problems. This advice, however, is not trying to replace the formal process of assessment and treatment in a clinical setting.

It is vital that you present these activities to your child as visual experiments or games. Do not use the terms "test" or "vision homework" as your child will feel pressure to perform and not want to participate. It is key that you set the level of each game to just the right point. The game should not be too easy where the child gets bored, nor should it be too challenging so that your child feels frustrated and discouraged. You want the games to be challenging enough that when your child "wins" they feel as though they have "worked for it." This can be more difficult than you think.

Although we could have dozens of games listed, I will discuss and give the rationale behind what I believe are the top five games, which will provide the parent/educator an informed idea of where their child is visually struggling. The information gathered can also allow the parent to participate more during the in-depth assessment with the doctor.

Vision games can either be about the hardware of the eye mechanics (oculomotor) or dealing more with the software of the visual system (visual processing.) If the game is the former, I will use the initials

"OM" (oculomotor), and if the game is more geared towards visual information processing skills, I will use the initials "VIP" to denote this. Most of these games can be done with children ages 7 and older and some six years old, depending on the child. If the child is less than six years old, it is best to take them for a regular eye examination first. If there are concerns detected, then have a more in-depth assessment done if required, depending on the results of the routine eye exam.

As an aside, even if your child is doing OK at school, annual routine eye exams are advised up until the age of 19 and every 1-2 years thereafter, depending on findings.

Visual Experiment #1 (OM): Suppression Check:

Do you have *magic vision*?

Background Information:

The phrase "simultaneously visually attend" refers to the ability to look in one place, but at the same time be visually attending somewhere else. As an example from the hearing world, imagine you are having a conversation with someone. At the same time, someone else in the room is having a separate conversation and mentions your name! You proceed to pretend to be listening to the original conversation, but now you are trying to *attend* or listen in on the other conversation. This is a great example of Divided Auditory Attention where I am hearing from one direction but *attending* to a completely different sound source. Visually Divided Attention is very similar. You are pointing your eyes at a particular spot, but you are visually *attending* to a different area.

This game is designed to determine two things. Firstly, can your child simultaneously visually attend? Secondly, does their brain use both eyes together at the same time?

Procedure:

1. Take a lollipop stick and draw a happy face on one end, large enough for your child to see. (These visual games do not have to be fancy!).

2. Set a target, (a large object, such as a giant stuffed animal or a TV screen), about 10-20 ft. (3m to 6m) away but at your child's eye level.

3. Hold the lollipop stick about 16 inches (40cm) from your child's nose, making sure it is about midway between their eyes and at their eye level, with the distant target on the same line of sight as the lollipop stick.

4. Ask your child to look at the face on the lollipop stick and tell you how many of the distant targets they see. (Hint: They should say "two").

5. Take note if they have a difficult time MAINTAINING fixation on the lollipop stick while trying to describe to you what is going on the background. Take note if their eyes water or get uncomfortable doing the game.

6. If your child sees one face, where they are looking, and two of the targets in the background, then say, "Well done, I think you have MAGIC VISION! Can you do it the other way around"?

7. Next, get your child to look at the distant target and hold the lollipop stick in the same place at near, as before. This time, ask them how many faces they see, (Hint: They should say "two").

8. If they see two faces, even if they are blurry, and one of the targets they are looking at (far away this time), then say something to the effect of, "Wow! You have Magic Vision far away and up close! Cool!" They will be very proud.

Sample Instructions:

"We are going to play a game called "Magic Vision." Do you want to play this game with me? I am going to get you to look at this lollipop stick at the smiley face I drew for you and then we will see how many of your big toys you see far away. OK? We call it "Magic Vision" because we want to see if you can look at the lollipop stick and without looking away from the lollipop stick, tell me how many of your big toys you see using your magic vision?

We will also do it the other way around. When you are looking at the big toy far away, I will hold up the lollipop stick. Without looking away from the big toy far away, we will ask you to try and tell me how many lollipop sticks you see."

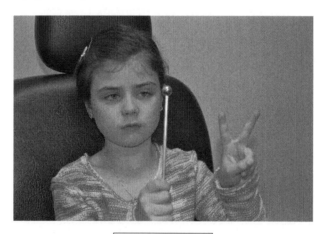

Magic Vision game

How to Interpret:

If your child has no issues, they should quickly and easily look at the lollipop stick and tell you that they see two of the far away toy, even if they may be fuzzy. If the child only sees ONE target far away during the test, then their brain is likely "suppressing" one eye. Always re-member that if both eyes are functioning relatively equally, the brain will prefer to use the information from BOTH eyes.

When you look at any object, other objects about 2-3 ft. in front or behind of what you are looking at, should be double and blurred. Now, it is surprising that our brain sees this as perfectly normal, and we are never consciously aware of it. So, if we only ever see one target in the background or the foreground in this test, it is a clear indication that there is a problem with the brain attending to the images equally from both eyes in the foreground and background relative to where we are fixating.

Possible Outcomes:

1. Your child sees one of what they are looking at and two of the targets they are not looking at = NORMAL result.
2. Your child only sees one of what they are looking at and only one image in the background or foreground = Likely SUPPRESSION of one eye.
3. Your child cannot look at the target and tell you what is going in the background without moving their eyes *to the background* = Likely poor PERIPHERAL AWARENESS skills or poor SIMULTANEOUS VISUAL PERCEPTION skills. This is not just "poor attention."

Visual Experiment #2 (OM): Peripheral Awareness Integrity:

Use "Magic Vision" to catch a bean bag without peaking.

Background Information:

This game is intended to gauge how well your child can maintain fixation on YOUR eyes when asked to catch a beanbag. If you have done Visual Experiment #1 above, you can extend the concept of their "Magic Vision" (which is referring to their Peripheral Awareness

Skills) to this experiment. If your child persistently has to sneak peeks to catch the beanbag during this game, it is a strong sign that they are not confident with their peripheral visual system. There may be an issue that needs further investigation.

Procedure:

1. Stand about 4-6ft apart from your child.
2. Instruct your child to look you in the eye at all times.
3. Throw a beanbag straight towards the middle of the body line of your child (Middle Throw) and see if they can catch it using their "Magic Vision" (i.e. they have to look at your eyes all the time, encourage them to blink as normal though.) Watch to see if they wait for the beanbag to hit their body first and then catch it. If this happens, they are a "Body Catcher". If they do this frequently, then likely Peripheral Visual Awareness is an issue.
4. Continue to ensure that your child is looking at you in the eyes at all times. If they catch the Middle Throw reasonably well, proceed to throw the beanbag from a shorter distance, within 1-2 ft., from your child's body, first on their left side and then on their right side, to see if they can catch it.

Proper central fixation using peripheral awareness to catch the beanbag. (i.e., "Magic Vision)

5. Continue to do the same steps but at a further distance, (3-4ft from the child, on the right and then on the left). This may require the child to move slightly in order to catch the beanbag. Observe your child's eye movements during these tasks, to see if they can maintain fixation on your eyes the whole time.

Child looking away from mom (i.e., not using peripheral awareness) to catch the beanbag. This indicates that there is maybe less confidence in this peripheral visual area.

6. You should keep a scorecard and show a score out of 10 throws for each scenario and create a grid-like record showing the direction of the beanbag and the number of times they were able to catch it, *without* looking away from your eyes.

Scorecard for "Beanbag Catch" game
Sample recording (child has to look you in the eye at all times!)

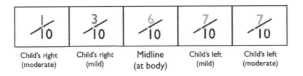

1/10	3/10	6/10	7/10	7/10
Child's right (moderate)	Child's right (mild)	Midline (at body)	Child's left (mild)	Child's left (moderate)

In this example, the child clearly has poor peripheral awareness more to THEIR right (this can be mentioned also to the doctor, it will help them in their assessment!)

Sample Instructions:

"We are going to play another game involving your "Magic Vision," OK? (Important: If they did not pass the first experiment, use the phrase, "We are going to play a game to see if you have special catching ability, OK?"). In this game, you have to look at my eyes all the time, so you have to use your side vision or "Magic Vision" to catch the beanbag, OK? The reason why you have to look me in the eye is to make sure that you don't "sneak a peek" at the beanbag when I throw it towards you. Try your best and we will keep score, OK? I will throw the beanbag ten times first straight at you, then to your right and then to your left. Sometimes I'll throw it closer to you, and sometimes I'll throw it further away from you. I will mix it up, so that you do not know which way I am going to throw the beanbag though, OK? You can move to catch the beanbag, you don't have to stand still, but you DO have to look me in the eye ALL THE TIME. If you feel that you HAVE to "sneak a peek" to catch the beanbag, that is ok, but just do your best, OK?"

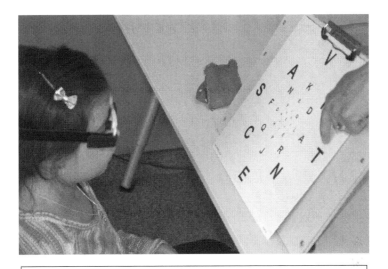

An example of one the exercises that the treating doctor may use to work on peripheral awareness skills. The child looks at the central (smaller) letter and without moving the eyes away from the central letter, the child has to tell the tester which letter they are pointing to WITHOUT moving the eye from the smaller central letter.

How to interpret:

If your child has good peripheral awareness, they should be able to get at least 7/10 in all positions. Concerns arise when results are anything less than 5/10. Borderline is 5-6/10. If your child's scores are more reduced on one side than the other, (for example, 3/10 on their right side, versus 9/10 on their left side), then bring this to the attention of the doctor. This may indicate difficulty with simultaneous visual attention ability, which is rooted in poor PA. This can be worked on in the in-office VT program with, for example, cards that use bigger letters in the periphery to train the child not to move their eyes but still "identify the letters" off to the side. This is an example of a PA exercise in VT (Called MacDonald cards) See pictures above for a visual.

Visual Experiment #3 (OM): Convergence Ability:

How close can you go to your nose, before you see two pens?

Background Information:

This simple test looks at how well your child's eyes move in together towards their nose, such as is required, for example, when reading. It is a simple screening test that can be done with a pen tip or a dot drawn on a lollipop stick.

Failure to demonstrate adequate Convergence usually occurs if the fusional mechanisms in the brain start to breakdown. However, if your child shows intact Convergence, they are almost guaranteed to have cortical fusion i.e., the brain is using both eyes at "the same time." This test is wonderfully simple but can give a wealth of information. It makes this game an excellent screening tool overall for anyone who wishes to know how their child's visual system is functioning. Of note, this is also a helpful screening test for infants. Convergence should be present in every infant older than four months. In an infant, you can move a toy towards them and just look to see if the eyes pull inward towards the nose at the same time (i.e. as a team.)

If the eyes cannot pull in properly, this condition is termed Convergence Insufficiency, or CI for short, and is one of the most common eye-teaming issues we encounter. Convergence is defined as both eyes being able to turn inwards towards the nose. Insufficiency means your child is unable or has difficulty doing the task without undue effort. So, CI means a problem pulling each eye inwards towards the nose, without undue effort, as one needs to do when reading.

Procedure:

1. Hold a pen or a lollipop stick with a dark spot drawn on it, (not too big, but not a pinprick either), in front of your child's eyes, about 30cm (12 inches) away.

2. Ask your child to look at the target (i.e., pen tip or the dot) and tell you if they see two of the pen/dot at any time.

3. SLOWLY move the target towards your child's eyes, staying on their "line of sight," and midway between the eyes. Watch their eyes while doing it, starting at about 30cm (about 12 inches) from the nose.

4. Both eyes should move smoothly and at the same speed towards the nose. Ideally, you should be able to move the target to within 3 inches (8cm) of the bridge of your child's nose, before your child either says, "I see two," or you visibly see one eye turn outwards (or more rarely inwards with some types of "strabismus.") It is essential that you look at a ruler or measuring tape before doing this test, so you can visualize the benchmark of 3 inches.

5. Watch your child for discomfort when doing the test. There should be no significant discomfort or watering of the eyes when doing this test. If either occurs, there is likely an issue.

Sample Instructions:

"In this vision experiment, we are going to see how well you can cross your eyes and move them towards your nose. I need you to look at this pen (or dot, if using a lollipop stick) and as I move it closer to you, tell me if you see two pens (dots). If it makes your eyes feel sore or it hurts your eyes, just let me know, OK?"

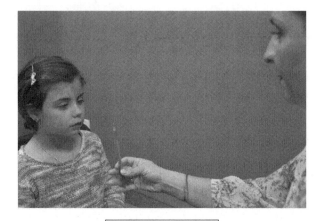

NPC testing by parent

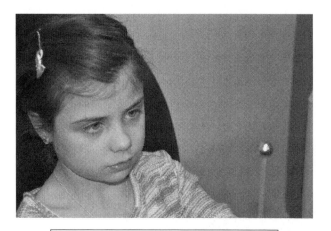

NPC testing by doctor using a "Wolff Wand" target

How to Interpret:

If your child can smoothly move each eye towards the bridge of their nose, closer than 3 inches (8 cm), then Convergence is likely intact. While doing the test, it is also essential to watch how your child reacts to the pen coming closer. Some may pass the exercise but feel really uncomfortable doing it. If a child has CI you often also see them

102

"rub their eyes a lot" more so with near tasks, which can often be mistaken as "allergies" in our clinical experience.

Possible Outcomes:

The following are various patterns you may observe:

1. Both eyes follow the target inwards in a smooth manner to the bridge of the nose or within 3 inches (8 cm) of the bridge of the nose without any discomfort reported = NORMAL result. To be sure, repeat 3 times.
2. Both eyes follow the target inwards in a smooth manner to the bridge of the nose or within 3 inches (8 cm) of the bridge of the nose with discomfort, (Look for "wincing" or narrowing of the eyelids or eyes watering.) = LIKELY A PROBLEM
3. Both eyes initially track the pen/target inwards towards the nose. However, before you reach the bridge of the nose (or within 3 inches (8 cm) from the bridge of the nose), one eye disengages and drifts outwards and does not continue to track the pen/target = ABNORMAL FINDING.

Hint: Your child may or may not say that they see two of the target, but the key is for you to *watch your child's eyes* as they track the pen inwards towards their nose. Most kids say they see two of the target. If their vision issue has been there for a long time, the brain learns and adapts by turning off the second image to avoid confusion. In the latter case, your child may not say they see two of the targets, but you still observe one of their eyes disengaging and failing to track the target inwards towards their nose.

Visual Experiment #4 (VIP): Visual Memory Game:

Can we remember what words look like?

Background Information:

Children with poor visual memory skills as a result of eye-teaming issues, often have problems remembering the details of what they have *just* seen or read. They will often default to spell a word "how it sounds" because despite even after seeing what the word looks like many times, they just cannot remember how actually to spell it *visually*! This is often to the frustration of the parent or educator.

This is because the brain will not store what does not look consistent. If every time the child looks at a word, it looks different, (sometimes clear, occasionally blurred, sometimes a single image, occasionally double – see images below), the brain will not bother trying to store the mental picture of the word. The brain is not sure what the word looks like - even though to the parent or the teacher, the word looks the same. To the child's brain, the word is continuously changing!

The aim of this game is to determine how well your child can "store what words look like." It tests to see if your child can visually recall words they have seen before and "know them when they see them." It also gives an indication of how well they can visually recall words they have not seen before or do not recognize. Both tasks involve visual memory skills but in different ways.

Blurry image

You can still see "20/20" and see like this. If a child has always "seen this way", they don't actually know any different and typically will not complain. In order to detect these visual issues, the eye doctor has to do very specific testing and pay attention to how the eyes move and team together in order to determine whether there is a problem. If your wish to get more information on eye teaming or eye focusing issues that can cause problems with reading, visit www.covd.org or www.vuetherapy.ca for more details. If your child skips lines when reading, avoids reading or gets frustrated quickly with reading, it is very likely a smart idea to have them assessed for eye teaming problems. If these issues are missed and left untreated, the effects on your child over time in terms of their academics can potentially be devastating.

Normal view

You can still see "20/20" and see like this. If a child has always "seen this way", they don't actually know any different and typically will not complain. In order to detect these visual issues, the eye doctor has to do very specific testing and pay attention to how the eyes move and team together in order to determine whether there is a problem. If your wish to get more information on eye teaming or eye focusing issues that can cause problems with reading, visit www.covd.org or www.vuetherapy.ca for more details. If your child skips lines when reading, avoids reading or gets frustrated quickly with reading, it is very likely a smart idea to have them assessed for eye teaming problems. If these issues are missed and left untreated, the effects on your child over time in terms of their academics can potentially be devastating.

Blurry and double image

Procedure:

1. Show your child the grade appropriate list of Fry words. (https://tinyurl.com/quaid-fry-ky) These are high frequency sight words used in the English language. (1st to 10th grade with 100 words per grade.) You can show the words by grade level. (Not applicable to children less than six years of age or less than grade 1.)

2. Using a blue pen, have your child circle 20 words, with four letters or more, that they believe they have seen before or think they know.

3. Using a red pen, ask your child to circle 20 words, with four letters or more, that they think they have not seen before or do not think they know.

4. Write each word circled in blue on a white blank index card, in large black print.

5. Write each word circled in red on a white blank index card, in large black print.

6. Scenario #1: Using the 20 "blue list" cue cards, (Do NOT show your child the word) ask your child to spell verbally each word after you read it out loud to them. Write down their spelling on the card for each word and mark it correct or incorrect. Remember not to show them the card. Do this for all the cards and record the score out of 20.

7. Scenario #2: Using 10 of the "red list" cue cards, show your child a word for 10 seconds, and then take it away. After your child sees the word, ask them to tell you what they think they saw. Write their word down on the cue card and mark it correct or incorrect. Record the score out of 10.

8. Scenario #3: Using the remaining 10 "red list" cue cards, show your child a word for 10 seconds as before, but this time you are going to give them a distraction while they are looking at the word. While showing each card, have your child count out loud from 1 to 10. They can stop counting once you have taken the card away. Ask the child to tell you what they think they saw. Write their word down on the cue card and mark it correct or incorrect. Do each card in a similar way. Record the score out of 10.

   You should now have one score out of 20 for the blue list of words and two scores out of 10 for the red list.

9. Ask your child if they know what the words "station" and "future" mean. If they do not know what the words mean, give them a sentence using each word to give them a context. It is important to note that we do not care at this point if the child can spell the words correctly, we are looking to see how they

approach *spelling them*. This test is applicable to grade 3 or higher.

10. Ask the child to spell these two words without seeing any cue cards. Record the results.

11. While attempting to spell these important words, observe the child to see if they are looking "into space," or whether they are moving their lips or looking as though they are "saying the word to themselves" in any way. These adaptations are crucial, as many children with poor visual memory will tend to "say the word to themselves" in order to try to sound it out. After all, if you cannot "picture the word," your only other is, "sound it out." Right? Hence, you see the mouth moving in a child who is spelling but *not* engaging their visual memory skills. Remember, the child with poor visual memory will spell future as, "fucher" or something close, and will spell station as, "stashun" or something close.

Sample Instructions:

*Do not tell your child it is a MEMORY game or they may try and memorize the words prior to the start of the game which will alter the results.

"We are going to play a game with some words, OK? It is not reading, but it is a word game. We are going to show you a list of words. To play the game, we need to circle 20 words with four letters or more that you know, with this blue pen. Then, we need to circle 20 words with four letters or more that you don't know, with this red pen. I can help you count how many you have circled, if you need help. We can then use these words to play the game, OK?"

How to interpret:

The blue list score (Scenario #1) represents the child's ability to recall words *they know when they see them written down*. In other words, they know them on a page but may have issues remembering how to spell them out loud without a visual cue. They should be able to get 20/20 of the blue list as they chose and circled those words that they thought they had seen before or thought they knew. If their score is less than 16/20 on the blue list, visual memory is likely an issue. If they score less than 12/20, visual memory is definitely an issue.

The red list score represents the child's ability to *assimilate new words*. This is measured in two ways, one that does not use an auditory block (Scenario #2 - not counting) and one using an auditory block (Scenario #3 - counting.) If a child has an excellent visual memory, the auditory block will usually have a minimal effect. If visual memory is weak however, the auditory block will likely have a devastating impact on the ability to recall what was just seen. When visual memory is reduced, the child relies on adaptations such as saying the sequence of letters to themselves in their head.

When you ask the child to count from 1 to 10 out loud, you are preventing the adaptations, thus forcing the brain to use visual memory alone. Most people will have a slightly lower score on this task of saying the numbers out loud. However, the difference will be dramatic in those with visual memory issues.

The first ten red-circled words used (Scenario #2's) score should be in the range of at least 6 or 7/10. This is because it involves immediate recall, and there is no auditory block being used. If this section is below 5/10, there is almost definitely a visual memory issue.

The second 10 red-circled words used (Scenario #3) score should be 5/10 or more and should always be within two of the first ten red-circled words score. For example, if the child scores 7/10 on the first ten red-circled words, then the child should score at least 5/10 on the second 10 red-circled words.

To Summarize *Normal* Results:

Scenario #1- Blue Words (20): At least 16/20 should be correct.

Scenario #2- Red Words (10- No Auditory Block): At least 7/10 should be correct.

Scenario #3- Red Words (10- Auditory Block): Within 2 tenths of the first red word score above and at least a total score of 5/10.

It is the *difference* between the two red word scores that are primarily of interest here. When Visual Memory is an issue, I have seen some children get 0/10 on Scenario #3 with the auditory block and 6/10 on Scenario #2 without the auditory block, as they have a tough time recalling what they see visually, when the speech system is occupied.

If they have adapted to be auditory learners with weak visual skills, then by having them say the numbers out loud they cannot use their stronger system (i.e., auditory.) You are forcing them to use the weaker visual system. They must remember what the word *looks like*, as they are busy counting they cannot say the letters to themselves or in their head.

Possible Outcomes:

Sample Scoring Chart Illustrating VM Issue:

Scenario #1 (Blue Words): 10/20 (Problem)

Scenario #2 (Red Words, No Auditory Block): 6/10 (OK)

Scenario #3: (Red Words, Auditory Block): 1/10 (Problem)

Sample Scoring Chart Illustrating Standard Results:

Scenario #1 (Blue Words): 18/20 (OK)

Scenario #2 (Red Words, No Auditory Block): 7/10 (OK)

Scenario #3: (Red Words, Auditory Block): 6/10 (OK)

Fry word list (100 per grade)

These lists are best as they are grade dependent and is recommended that the list 1 be done by end of grade 1, list 2 by end of grade 2 and list 3 by end of grade 3 (see the TinyUrl link below) etc. Lists are shown via the link below in PDF downloadable format from grades 1-10

https://tinyurl.com/quaid-fry-ky

Visual Experiment #5 (VIP): Copying Game:

How fast can we copy words from on page to another at near?

Background information:

This test can easily be used by a parent at home as a quick screening. This game is merely to see how fast your child can copy words. It is not a test of spelling, as they can see the words written in front of them. Ideally, your child should be in grade one (age 6) or older. This screening game is based on a formal test called the WOLD Sentence Copying Test. A doctor can do this in greater detail at their office.

Copying text from one page to another involves a lot of visual skills. The child must be able to look at the word and hold the image of the word in their mind while they copy the letters to another page. They also have to be able to maintain their eyes in an inward position to look at near in addition to being able to keep the words clear when doing this task. This is difficult for someone with visual skills issues.

If visual memory is a problem or there is an eye-teaming issue, you will often see the child moving their eyes many times more than usual back and forth from the print to the page - often several times for only one word. Most of us should make roughly one eye movement per word (look at the word once), and successfully write it out in one try. Kids with excellent visual memory can often grab two or three words in one glance and copy them out successfully onto the page.

When doing this task with your child, please do not call it a test!

Merely state that it is a "visual experiment" to see how their eyes move. Your task when they are copying the text is to see how many letters per minute they can copy. It would also be of value, without being obvious, if you count how many "peeks " they make when copying each word.

I would use a timer on your phone or a stopwatch for this experiment. At one-minute intervals, make a note of how many letters they have copied to that point. The text used should have approximately has 110 letters (29 words) in total. I would give your child as long as they need to copy the whole text. The reason for this is that in many cases of visual dysfunction, the child may start out quickly in the first minute and then begin to slow down. As you record your child's letters per minute, watch for signs of fatigue. You may also see your child looking closer at the page as well, as time goes on. Remember, this is a difficult, sometimes frustrating task, for someone with visual skills issues. Create a grid similar to the one below to record how many letters are copied per minute and note any fatigue effects.

WOLD sentence copying test

Sample of Normal Results Grade 3

	Letters per Minute
Minute 1	
Minute 2	
Minute 3	

(Norm approx. 40 letters / minute*)

Procedure:

1. Set your child up with a blank piece of lined paper and a pencil or a pen (whichever they prefer). Make sure you have a recording sheet to record the number of letters copied per minute.
2. Have them copy a paragraph consisting of 29 words, 110 letters, including one comma and one full stop.
3. Record how many eye movements or peeks your child makes while copying the paragraph. Also, record how many letters per minute they copied. (So, pay attention to your timer!)
4. Make notes of how close your child is getting to the print and if they are copying with "Heavy Small Print" or "Large Spidery Print". Also take notes, if your child can print successfully on the lines. This is a crucial piece. Visual skills issues often result in simply not writing "on the line" accurately. This issue alone is often a telltale sign of visual skills issues.

Sample instructions:

"We are going to do a vision experiment OK? In this experiment, we are going to see what your eyes do when you are copying words. It

---

* If your child goes 20% longer per minute than expected, there is likely an issue. So based on the above example, any minute with 48 letters or more likely indicates an issue. Since there are 29 words, if we assume a maximum of "two peeks" per word, also more than 60 peeks is likely an issue also.

would be helpful to me if you could copy these words on this sheet to this page. Do not rush. Try to copy the words at the same speed you would at school. We want to get an idea of how your eyes move when you are copying things. If your eyes get too tired just let me know OK?"

To learn more about the Wold test and to see a sample, please use the custom link below.

https://tinyurl.com/quaid-wold

How to Interpret:

Results that would indicate an issue:

1. Your child is copying at a rate of more than 20% or more outside of expected letters per minute. (i.e., longer than 3 minutes likely an issue – longer than 3 ½ minutes definitely an issue.)
2. Your child is getting close to the page while copying.
3. Your child is peeking at one word multiple times.
4. Your child is copying fewer and fewer letters per minute as time goes on.
5. Your child does not complete the task and says, "I cannot do this mom/dad." Do not force them to finish, but do note that just doing the task frustrated them.
6. Your child is rubbing their eyes when doing the task, frequently looking away from the print or getting distracted easily.

Asking your child a few simple questions after they have finished the vision experiment will help to gain insight into what they noticed visually while doing the task. Questions such as:

1. Was the print *perfectly* clear all the time?
2. Did you see the letters or words move or look like they were getting jumbled on the page?
3. How did your eyes feel when you were copying?

SUMMARY:

These five vision games should give you valuable information as to whether your child has visual skills issues. They are very helpful in determining whether your child's brain is ignoring one eye or paying attention to one eye much more than the other. The results of these games will likely reveal poor convergence ability, (pulling the eyes towards the nose), tracking issues (poor peripheral awareness), poor near point focusing (accommodation), and poor visual memory skills. These tests should also tell you if there is a "phonetic pattern" tendency in the child's spelling approach.

Parents, if you remember nothing else from this book, remember this. If a child continues to spell a word by "how it sounds" and cannot recall "what it looked like" despite you showing the word to them several times, then it is highly likely that they cannot use their visual skills appropriately. A persistent phonetic spelling approach, even as the child ages, by itself, indicates poor visual memory.

I firmly believe that a massive proportion of children labeled as learning disabled are not having their visual skills assessed beyond "20/20." Parents and educators are not given enough detail to detect and triage the issues. As reading involves the child moving their eyes inwards and downwards, while looking from side to side and then, when coming to the end of the line, having to make a very complex eye movement back to the start of the next line, this places complex demands on the eyes and brain. This is nothing like reading 6 or so letters (not words) from 20 feet away from an eye chart during a routine eye examination.

It never ceases to amaze me how often children will state when we show them a video of print coming in and out of focus or drifting in and out of double images that they "thought everyone saw that way." Parents often become emotional when they understand the truth and realize their child has an issue and was not being "lazy" or "not trying hard enough." They also recognize that these visual skills issues can not be helped with more tutoring. Visual rehabilitation by a team of eye care professionals dedicated to this area is often a lifeline for such children. Yes, we need all the professional disciplines partnering together to fix these cases, and usually, several components are required. However, make no mistake that visual skills are high on the list. Sadly, right now, visual skills are hardly ever discussed. This has to change.

"Children must be taught how to think,
not what to think."

MARGARET MEAD

STARTING THE JOURNEY OF VISION ASSESSMENT

We have previously discussed the fact that a routine eye examination and a more in-depth visual assessment (Visual Skills Assessment or VSA) are entirely different assessments. Regular eye examinations most certainly have their place and are critical for the detection of customary eye conditions and diseases such as glaucoma, macular disease, and retinal detachments. They also result in a proper prescription for eyeglasses or contact lenses, for example, so that one can see clearly. However, when the patient has an eye teaming issue or a visual processing issue, a very different and more functional approach is required.

In North America, accredited schools have an Optometry School in some twenty-five universities. However, very few offer programs for eye doctors that provide any structured formal training in the area of Vision Therapy. An organization outside of the accredited university system that has many faculty members of many schools on its board (including me) has spearheaded a formal certification process called the "FCOVD process." This Fellow of the College of Optometrists in Vision Development designation is conferred on the doctor once they have demonstrated competence to the level of Board Certified (or Fellowship trained.) It is training over and above what the eye doctor learns during their regular training and is desirable to demonstrate a deep understanding of this often-challenging area. Even for myself, after having trained in two countries in optometry, having attained a Ph.D, and a post-doctorate in Vision Science, the FCOVD process was still very challenging to go through. It challenged me to think about my training in a different light and think about it in a more functional way.

Diagnosing diseases of the eye are vital of course, but we have not concentrated enough on visual skills assessment. Now, this may sound like an odd statement, but at every age of life, especially in childhood, the prevalence of functional disorders far outweighs the incidence of all eye diseases combined! If you add up all the eye-teaming disorders in the general population (i.e., strabismus, amblyopia, convergence disorders, accommodative disorders, tracking disorders, etc.), we are talking at least 1 in 10 people struggle with these conditions. This number jumps dramatically in the learning difficulty and concussion population where it can be 6-8 in 10.

To detect there is a preferred sequence of tests that should be undertaken. Some of these tests can be done quickly during a routine eye examination. In this chapter, we will assume that the routine exam was found to be normal. Of note, over 80% of the cases that come to our clinic for assessment have had a routine exam done in the past year and had not had any issues flagged.

Therefore, a child with a normal eye exam but has an IEP/learning difficulty that is rooted in reading should have a more in-depth visual skills assessment.

However, basic eye teaming tests that can and should be done in the routine eye examination should include:

1. Basic Case History: The most important aspect here is for the doctor to ask about the child's READING performance in school. Topics such as the IEP, grades, and the significant disconnect between reading skills and what the child understands when being read to discussed. Questions such as, "Does the child take an inordinate amount of time to copy things from the board?" are helpful. Do they need extra time for exams? How is their spelling?" give significant clues.

2. Visual Acuity: This notices how the child reads the letter chart at a distance and also at near even if they do get "20/20". Questions to use include, "Did each eye read the letters easily and quickly or did the child have to *really work to get it*?" Did they narrow their lids or have to move their head to an odd angle to see the letters?" It is not just about whether they "got 20/20," it is also about how much work they had to expend to get that "20/20." If the eyes have different performances, this is an issue by itself – especially if this cannot be corrected with lenses.

3. Eye Alignment: This asks the question, "Do the eyes point in the same place at the same time?" The eye doctor can do various tests, (i.e., cover test, Maddox rod, etc.) to determine this. Gently ask the doctor, "Are my child's eyes precisely aligned?" A simple yes or no should be the answer.

4. Depth Perception: This is a crucial assessment and mainly refers to whether your child can see in 3D appropriately. This is not an all or nothing measure; it is a scale between zero and ten. Your child might have 6/10 depth perception (with 0 being none and 10 being age-appropriate.) Ask the doctor what number your child has on a 0-10 scale. If it is less than 10, this is a problem. The doctor can use a random-dot test (like the magic eye book pictures) with some 3D glasses to test for this.

5. Near Point of Convergence (NPC): This test is so simple that a parent can do it at home. Use a pen tip or your finger and have the child follow this target towards their nose. Observe your child for two things. Do both eyes move smoothly inwards and at the same speed as you move towards the bridge of the nose? Does one eye "quit" and stop moving in towards the nose? The child may or may not see double when one eye quits but *watch the eyes*. The result should be that you get fairly close to the bridge of the nose before one eye quits turning in (technically <3 inches (8cm) from the nose bridge is a normal result.) Also,

if the result is normal but the child is uncomfortable doing the test, this is also a concern.

The proper result should be that the patient is able to easily follow the pen tip/target towards the bridge of the nose without one eye quitting. When one reads, the eyes have to turn inwards towards the nose. If they cannot do this with a pen tip, they will not be able to sustain that inward eye posture when reading.

6. Cycloplegic Examination (the "drops.") Based on our 2013 publication, you will see that I do not recommend using the drops for *all* children. This is somewhat controversial. What I mean by this, is that not every child with a reading based issue or an IEP in school requires the use of the drops for the eye examination.

   The drops are used for individuals who are long-sighted (their distance vision is reasonably normal, but they have to work to make it clear at near.) Using the drops to dilate the pupil and relax the internal focusing muscles that may be over-working is crucial to assess more so in cases of reading difficulties. This allows the doctor to realize the full extent of the long-sightedness issue. Any results using the drops of over +1.25DS, should be considered for at least partial correction, especially if the child reports, "Things go blurry sometimes when I read."

7. Retinal Examination: In this test, the doctor looks at the physical eye (front and back of the eye, retina) to determine whether or not any pathology or disease is present. This is usually done in all eye examinations. In our experience, in vision-based learning difficulty cases, the physical exam is typically normal. The issue is not a disease but a visual skills or functionally based issue.

So, once you have the routine examination, kindly ask your eye doctor to run over the seven tests listed above, to see if any issues arise. Even if all seven areas above are normal, I would also proceed as a parent, to fill out both questionnaires in our chapter, "Empowering Parents and Educators." It is based on a level 1 NIH funded study, called the CITT study, or Convergence Insufficiency Treatment Trial. I would ask your child each question (if they are age six or above) and ask them to respond with the options presented. When complete, add up the columns of answers.

A typical result from a routine eye exam *does not* automatically means there are no visual processing issues, or more subtle eye-teaming concerns. This is a key statement. Based on our 2013 paper, having an IEP alone puts you at a very high likelihood of having an eye-teaming issue (greater than 84%.)

Another important tip for parents is to watch your child when they read. Watch their posture, watch if they adopt odd head angles, watch if they start to cover or close one eye, watch if they have to use a finger to help them track. These are all critical points for the doctor to be aware of when you discuss case history. If possible, video record your child reading and writing, I find this information invaluable when I am doing more in-depth visual skills assessment.

Remember one simple fact. If someone says, "My child sees 20/20" just simply respond: "Great, what about the other 94% of the visual system?" That usually starts a conversation.

"Most of the important things in the world have been accomplished by people who kept on trying when there seemed to be no help at all."

DALE CARNEGIE

LOOKING DEEPER UNDER THE HOOD

Similar to the car analogy, when you are learning to drive a stick shift, the actions of changing gears are anything but automatic! If someone even spoke to you while you were learning, you would get upset. It is like this in the VT room in the early stages when we are showing the patient initially how to align their eyes. We try to get the patient's proper alignment going by using equipment - some computerized and some non-computerized free space equipment. In the beginning, this can be hard work.

After more experience driving with a stick shift, though, the driver finds the motions become much more natural and needs less concentration to be successful. In the clinic, we help the patient practice their alignment techniques with an expanding range of situations. We change the stimulus and, the patient has to maintain alignment. Over time, our goal is to get them to a place where they can change the alignment themselves and demonstrate control over the system. This usually happens about halfway through the process.

What happens in between the initial awkwardness of learning something new and the relaxed, confident movements of experience is called "loading." This is a term used in therapy all the time. "Loading" is what happens between when the patient initially learns a technique and the practiced expanding ranges under which that technique can be performed.

When driving, you may be confronted with more challenging tasks than just the mechanics of driving. Experiences like watching the road, looking for traffic lights, and paying attention to other drivers on the road, can result in the brain pushing the motor task of driving to a subconscious level. This is the level we aim to achieve with Vision Therapy. Like breathing, eye-teaming should be part of who we are, not something we have to consciously *think about* doing.

A general flow in VT can be simplified to the following sequence. Potentially, each stage overlaps.

1. Gross Motor Stage: Ensuring that the child has proper balance and body awareness in space and has no retained reflexes that might cause difficulty in the child sitting "still". Occupational Therapy, (OT) would get involved if required.

2. Equalization of Monocular Visual Skills Stage: Making sure both eyes can track accurately and can refocus from a distance to near, at equal speeds.

3. Bi-ocular Stage: (This may need to use prisms in the VT room, which are special lenses make the patient see two separate images, one above the other, with one image coming from each eye.) Testing to see if the child can see two images and control their separation, by either diverging or converging the eyes (i.e., moving the eyes inwards towards the nose or outwards.) The fact that the child can see two images gives them biofeedback, as to whether they are doing the exercise correctly. If one image, for example, disappears, the patient knows one eye has "turned off."

4. Fusion Stage (Levels 1, 2 and 3): Starting with 2D images using an overlap of dissimilar images, moving to an overlap of similar images and then progressing to 3D images (non-randot and then rondot stereograms.) This is similar to the 3D image stereo books and posters that were very popular years ago. Many people can see the hidden images. What does that mean? (See these webpages for more examples)
https://en.wikipedia.org/wiki/Autostereogram
https://en.wikipedia.org/wiki/Random_dot_stereogram

5. Advanced Fusional Stage: Fusing images in 3D (both real images and random dot stereograms) while the images are moving and/or changing both rapidly and slowly in separation, changing the demand on the eyes to keep the images fused.

6. Visual Perceptual Skills Stage: This stage can, and often is, introduced as early as Stage 2 above and is "sprinkled" into every stage almost. It refers to the exercises/techniques designed to build the patients ability to recall what has been seen (i.e., visual memory skills) and also pay visual attention to subtle differences in visual patterns (i.e., visual discrimination skills.) This is to prepare them for the ultimate act of reading, and more. Reading involves both rapid recognition of sequences of letters and being able to retain what has been seen!

7. Development of RAN (Rapid Automated Naming) Function Stage: RAN function refers to the ability to do a task and being able to do it quickly, efficiently - almost without thinking. Examples of such exercises would be Kirshner arrows and rapid flash presentation of word-based cue cards. For example, there are lists of words of some 100-120 words (for example Dolch word lists) representing over 60% of all print on a page. If you could get them down on a RAN technique, you would have improved both written and reading based performance potentially by *at least* 60%.

Below is a table that briefly outlines the most common oculomotor and VIP metrics that we monitor throughout therapy to ensure gains are being realized.

Table 1A below (Oculomotor Metrics, "the hardware")

Name of Test	Brief description	Normal values
Near point Convergence (NPC)	How far can the patient move a target (i.e., pen) towards their nose before they see double or one eye disengages?	<3 inches (8cm) from the bridge of the nose.
Stereopsis / Depth perception	How well can the patient see in 3D?	40" arc or better at distance and near.
Amplitude of Accommodation (monocular and binocular values)	How near can the patient bring 20/30 print and keep it clear?	Hofstetter's formula (18.5-1/3 of age) as an average value in "dioptres".
Vergence ranges and vergence facility	How well can the eyes move inwards and outwards whilst maintaining fusion?	15cpm at near (12BO/3BI prism) and 2:1 ratio of PFVs to NFVs.
Unilateral and alternating cover tests	Checks alignment status of the eyes at distance and near.	Patient should be non-strabismic at distance and near with no strain tendencies inward or outward.
Fixation disparity	Even if eyes are aligned, are they under STRAIN in order to sustain alignment overall?	No fixation disparity slips at distance and near.
Worth 4 dot test	Checks for suppression or double vision.	Seeing 4 targets with red/green glasses on.
Saccadic eye movement testing (DEM testing or King-Devick testing)	How efficiently do the eyes move in terms of tracking horizontally and vertically?	>50th percentile horizontally and vertically in terms of tracking.
Visual Acuity at distance and near	How clearly does the patient see at distance and near?	20/20 with each eye separately and together at least.

Name of Test	Brief description	Normal values
Accommodative facility testing (monocular and binocular, MAF and BAF testing)	How quickly and efficiently can the patient change focus from distance to near and vice versa?	10 cycles per minute at least using +/-2DS testing with both one eye at a time and both eyes together.
Hess Test	To determine if the eyes are aligned in the 9 cardinal positions of gaze and if there are any "undershoots or overshoots"	Complete alignment in all 9 positions of gaze

Table 1B below (Visual Processing Metrics, "the software")

Name of Test	Brief description	Normal values (Scored relative to age-matched normative data)
TOSWRF-2 testing (Test Of Silent Word Reading Fluency 2nd Edition)	How quickly and efficiently can the patient read?	50th percentile ideally (i.e. middle of the pack).
TVPS test battery (Test of Visual Perceptual Testing)	Seven areas that look at skills such as visual memory and visual discrimination.	50th percentile ideally (i.e. middle of the pack).
DTVP-A (Developmental Test of Visual Perception, Adults)	Similar to the TVPS but for patients age 20 or older.	50th percentile ideally (i.e. middle of the pack).
WOLD sentence copying test	To determine copying speed of child at near	Results in percentiles
Gardiner / Jordan Reversal Test	To determine frequency of reversals and whether it is normal for age or not	Results in percentiles

In our clinic, we re-assess all or a selection of these metrics every 12 sessions of therapy, to measure the gains. If progress is slow for two checkpoints in a row (baseline data does not count as a checkpoint), we stop therapy and give the patient a break. We then try to figure out if there is any missed confounding factors and decide how to proceed. If gains have occurred and the patient is at the MRP (Maximum Rehabilitative Potential) Stage, we graduate the patient from the VT, as they have done well.

It is essential to use a scientific approach using quantifiable data to measure progress. We have published data in a medical journal showing a correlation between several of these metrics, to poor reading. This is in addition to data showing a cause-and-effect relationship between the two. This data supports the notion that if you treat one, the other typically improves.

When a child has successfully finished the process and graduates from the VT program, they often thank us before leaving. My good friend and colleague Dr. Dan Cunningham, always states to the child, "No, *you* that did all the work, not me. We just showed you the way." I could not put it better. We believe the child deserves to *own their success* because the child has likely experienced many failures prior to their time with us. Now, with their hard work, it is genuinely something that can empower them and unlock their potential to move forward. It is a beautiful gift that they can look at down the road and say "*I* did that. *I* succeeded at that difficult task."

That is a powerful statement. The vast majority who complete VT in our clinic (north of 84%) get to at least grade and age-appropriate levels of reading within 6-12 months. As well, a significant gain in reading has been seen in over 50% of the patients in VT as early as the second checkpoint (24 sessions.) The average patient takes around 48 sessions (+/-12 sessions) to complete Vision Therapy.

> For a comprehensive view of this topic, click or copy the following TinyUrl to see the PDF of Dr. Quaid and Dr. Cunningham's poster.
> https://tinyurl.com/quaid-covd-poster

Scheduled progress evaluations also check that the oculomotor aspects are improving. This is measured using specific equipment, ranging from prisms and lenses, to specialized equipment like a Visagraph III (see image below.) This piece of equipment is useful in recording in real-time, eye movements when reading, and can give invaluable information statistically. We use this to help parents understand why "despite seeing 20/20" the child still has issues reading. It is data that guides us. Only as recently as 2008 NIH funded CITT study have we started to scratch the surface from a data standpoint to confirm that these interventions are highly valuable as part of a multi-disciplinary approach to therapy.

See the following YouTube clip to see the Visagraph in action
https://tinyurl.com/quaid-lcr

I am proud to say that our clinic and our team are part of that movement to collect data and share it in peer-reviewed journals, and reference textbooks. That is in addition to presenting data at conferences all over the world.

Using the metrics presented in the table at the start of this chapter, this represents the minimal level of care that should be provided to any patient and family participating in a doctor-supervised VT program.

The doctor and the team should provide metrics to show that therapy is or is not effective.

"Without data, you are just another opinion."

W. EDWARDS DEMINS, DATA SCIENTIST

UNDERSTANDING THE IEP

JENNY FOUNTAIN

I remember the day my eldest child came into the world. The overwhelming joy I felt was punctuated by a palpable sense of relief. He had finally arrived! He had ten fingers, ten toes and looked the picture of health. I spent hours daydreaming about his future. I remember singing him to sleep and telling him that he would move mountains one day. There was nothing he couldn't do!

It had been a very stressful and uncertain pregnancy for me. Being a first-time mother is always an anxious time. Every ache or pain provokes worry. Routine checkups are important. They bring reassurance from expert physicians, who explain that what you are feeling is perfectly normal and routine. During my second trimester, however, the obstetricians in the province of Ontario went on strike to protest government cuts to healthcare. Due to insurance regulations, my family physician would only provide my prenatal care until the fifth month of pregnancy, and after that, I was on my own.

In the first trimester, my family doctor indicated that I needed a caesarean and I was at higher risk because I have cerebral palsy. As the obstetrician strike dragged on, my anxiety went through the roof. News channels reported that pregnant women would be turned away at all Ontario emergency rooms and possibly rerouted to the United States. Those who were able were encouraged to make home birthing plans. I was a young first-time mother. My pregnancy was considered high-risk, but I also knew that my husband and I would never be able to cover the cost of delivering a child in the United States. Thankfully, in answer to prayer, the strike ended in my eighth month. However, my relief at finally having a proper doctor was short lived. At that first appointment, it was discovered that I had developed gestational diabetes and required an extremely restrictive diet. I was required to test my blood sugar before and after every meal. Did I mention I have a severe needle phobia? It would take me close to 45 minutes to gather the courage to test my blood. I was a bundle of nerves. I couldn't wait to reclaim my pre-pregnancy body and order my worries to take a hike!

Fast forward four years. My son, now very bright, was extraordinarily hyperactive and had difficulty following rules. It seemed every day was a fresh opportunity for the teachers at his preschool to report on the negative things he did. I didn't blame them, but I was beginning to wonder if he would ever grow out of his busy personality that pushed everyone's buttons. The phrase "acts as if driven by a motor" was an understatement. He couldn't sit still. I remember watching him change seats at the breakfast table 47 times, *yes 47 times*! Just watching him was exhausting.

As Kindergarten approached, my anxiety resurfaced. Would my son be ready? Would his teachers be ready? As a teacher myself, I knew that many of his behaviours were red flags in the classroom. I tried several times to get help but always met resistance. The *professionals* suggested, *wait until he starts school*. He was already having trouble at daycare, yet somehow school was supposed to change the equation magically?

I was approached by his teacher many times during that first month of school. As I expected, she had concerns regarding my son's progress. She suggested we meet to discuss her observations. Being a teacher, I have always had courageous conversations about students with their parents. This time it was *my* child. Yes, I already knew there were issues and I had been actively searching for answers, yet I still remember wanting to hide under a table when she asked, "*Have you thought about medication?*" Eventually, he was given medication and placed upon a behavioural IEP, or Individual Education Plan. Despite my teacher training, I remember feeling that I had somehow failed my son.

Most parents are in a certain amount of shock when told their child is struggling and requires an IEP. Anxiety or disbelief are understandable reactions to the news that your child's learning is not unfolding as expected. The future that you have carefully planned for your child is suddenly at risk. We love our children. We are not hiding our perfect kids at home and sending the second string to school. Please try to remember, when discussing your child's needs with teachers, doctors, or specialists, these professionals genuinely want the best for your child. Resist the urge to feel, as I did, that this is all your fault. Keep the lines of communication with the school open and remain positive. This is especially critical if you had a negative school-experience yourself as a child. The rest of this chapter is meant to introduce parents, grandparents, and guardians to the IEP process. I trust you will find the information helpful as you to navigate the IEP experience with less anxiety, greater confidence, and peace of mind.

Once a teacher identifies that a student is struggling, he or she will begin having regular conversations with parents. Teachers will often ask a variety of questions about your child during these initial conversations. Does your child like to read at home? Does she play with Lego? Do you notice if your child becomes increasingly frustrated when completing homework, or tasks that sustain mental effort? When was your child's most recent eye examination, or hearing test completed? These questions may seem strange or intrusive, at first, but rest assured they are crucial. The answers, combined with teacher observations at school, will build a blueprint of your child's unique strengths and abilities.

Every school board has their benchmarks but, at my board for example, if a student receives two consecutive terms of failing grades (R level), a School-Based Team (SBT) meeting is usually scheduled. The SBT is made up of educators and support staff who work regularly with your child. Often the team involves the classroom teacher, Learning Support Teacher, and the Principal. At this initial meeting, the team will study data that has been collected on your child. This usually includes previous report cards, diagnostic tests, unit tests, daily work samples, anecdotal observations, medical documentation, psychological assessments and anything else that shows evidence of your child's strengths and areas of need. In Ontario, after reviewing all the available evidence, the SBT may refer your child's case to an IPRC (Identification Placement and Review Committee) upon written request by the parent. The school principal may also initiate an IPRC review after giving written notice to parents. Even if there is not enough evidence for an IPRC, the SBT could also place your child on a non-identified IEP with your consent.

The IEP

An IEP or Individual Education Plan is an official document that identifies your child's unique abilities and needs. It is helpful to consider an IEP as a written plan for your child's learning. It contains a great deal of valuable information about your child in addition to outlining instructional practices and assessment methods. The IEP is a working document that is not set in stone. As your child demonstrates mastery of an expectation or begins a new unit of study, the IEP will require revision. The IEP must be reviewed at the beginning of a new term, or school year. I like to remind parents that the IEP is a helpful tool for all essential stakeholders. The IEP not only outlines your child's abilities and academic needs, in one convenient document, but it keeps everyone answerable for your child's learning, including your child! It is helpful when everyone who works with your child can contribute to the development of the IEP. My son's IEP, for example, was created in consultation with myself, medical experts, classroom teachers, and valuable educational partners. I also discussed the document with him. Older students, those aged 16 and older in Ontario, are encouraged to participate in the IEP process. Regardless of who is involved in the creation of your child's IEP, if it is to be effective, the document should contain specific information:

- Your child's academic strengths and learning needs.

- Current assessment data that accurately shows your child's strengths and needs.
- Relevant medical tests, or health information, that may have an impact on learning or behaviour.
- A list of subject areas requiring modifications and/or accommodations for your child.
- Your child's most recent report card marks and/or current achievement level in a course or subject.
- A yearly goal for your child.
- A list of specific curriculum expectations that your child is expected to complete for each reporting period, or term, in the current school year.
- A list of assessment methods that your child's teacher will use when evaluating your child's progress.
- An explanation of the strategies the teacher will use to report your child's progress throughout the term.
- If your child is 14 years of age, or older, a transition plan should be included (unless the exceptionality is giftedness).

The IEP process in Ontario is guided by Ministry Regulation 181/98 and may differ somewhat in your corner of the world, but will essentially follow five basic stages:

1. Gather your data
2. Chart the course
3. Build the document
4. Put it in motion
5. Check-in

Gather Your Data

Your child's IEP will now take shape. The team will look at your child's academic history. This includes reviewing an IEP from the previous grade, or the decision of the IPRC. If this is your child's first IEP, then data can be gathered from your child's current teacher, his previous teachers, as well as information stored in your child's OSR (Ontario Student Record) or academic file. The IEP team will also ask for input from parents, support staff, medical professionals, and in the case of older students, your child. I was surprised at how much my son understood about his learning challenges. His input was constructive and gave him a voice. The team will also gather anecdotal observations from your child's classroom teacher, work samples and may invite other professionals from the community to observe.

Outside support is sometimes warranted if additional tests are required to get a complete picture of your child's abilities and struggles. Tests that your child has taken outside of the school are equally critical. At the first sign of academic difficulty, it is vital, as we have read in previous chapters, to schedule a proper vision screening and a hearing test. I took my son in for yearly eye exams throughout elementary and secondary school. He always scored better than 20/20. I never dreamed that his struggles might be due to an eye-teaming issue. I didn't even know that FCOVD trained eye doctors existed!

Chart the Course

First and foremost, the IEP process is a team effort! Once the team has gathered the necessary information, the responsibility for building your child's IEP will extend to those who work closely with your child. This is generally the classroom teacher or special education teacher. Support staff, occupational therapists, speech and language teachers should be part of the direction setting process. Remember, collaboration at this stage is critical! Sharing observations about your child will help the IEP team understand your child's abilities, struggles, and behaviours. People who know their likes, dislikes, fears, and frustrations can make valuable recommendations about strategies that have been successful in the past. Remember, creating an IEP is a process! As your child's IEP team moves toward the development phase, they need rich data about your child's abilities which also includes information gathered during an IPRC.

In Ontario, the school principal is responsible for ensuring that all planning, coordinating and development is completed within 30 days. IPRC recommendations are included in the final IEP, and it is reviewed at least once every reporting period. The special education teacher for your child's school can provide diagnostic assessments and suggestions about modifications, accommodations, specialized supports or equipment. Parents have a critical role in setting direction too. It is vital that you remain open to sharing information about your child with the school. You know your child best. Sharing your child's likes and dislikes with the school is very helpful. Every student has a motivator. My son would always work for Lego or technology. His IEP had these incentives built in as instructional strategies which helped to motivate him while simultaneously capitalizing on his natural strengths.

The reason for creating the IEP must also appear in the document. The reason for an IEP may be that the student was identified as exceptional by IPRC. Not all students who have an IEP are considered exceptional by IPRC, but if your child requires modifications or accommodations to be successful in the classroom, then an IEP is needed.

Personal information is always included in the IEP document. This information includes your child's name, age, student identification number, the date, school, principal's name and the names of any other teachers. If there was an IPRC, this date would be included, as well as your child's exceptionality and placement.

Where your child is placed is dependent on his or her needs and the options at your child's school. Most schools will endeavour to keep your child in the regular classroom, with supports, whenever possible. As a teacher, I always try to reassure parents that having an IEP does not mean that your child will be in a special education classroom. Most students stay in their regular classes with extra supports.

The IEP will list your child's specific strengths and areas of need. It is essential to know your child's preferred learning style. Is your child a visual learner? Or does your child prefer to work with their hands? It doesn't make much sense to lecture to a kinesthetic learner! If your child was diagnosed with vision issues or struggles with visual memory, this is vital to communicate.

Build the Document

Your child's IEP will identify all subject areas your child will be taught. The decision is then made whether to include modifications or accommodations, modifications and accommodations, or alternative programming.5 The teacher responsible for each subject area should create the IEP for that subject. For example, if your child requires an IEP for reading and science your child's literacy teacher would develop the IEP expectations for the reading subject page and the science teacher would complete the science section of the document.

Accommodations and modifications are frequently used words in the world of education. Sometimes it is challenging to keep each term clear in your mind. Accommodations and modifications are changes to *what* your child learns and *how* they will learn it.

Accommodations describe changes or supports, for your child that does not affect the *content* of what your child is learning. Accommodations are changes in *how* your child learns. These could include but are not limited to, specific teaching strategies, changes to the learning environment, special technology or equipment.

Teaching Strategies	Changes to Environment	Technology
• Large-print desk copies • Repeating instructions aloud • Visual instructions • Provide extra time	• Quiet place to work • Study Carrel • Write tests in another room	• Laptops • Magnifiers • Whisper phones

A *modification* is a change to the curriculum content or, essentially, a difference in *what* your child is learning. This might include, focusing upon fewer expectations at your child's current grade level, or using curriculum expectations from a different grade. A modification could be alternative test questions or alternative assignments. Modifications are intended to make learning more accessible to your child.

One section of the IEP focuses on teaching strategies and assessment methods your child's teacher will use. Most of the teaching strategies and assessment methods outlined in an IEP are simply good teaching practice!

Teaching strategies are the practices your child's teacher will use when teaching curriculum content. Most parents of my generation grew up in classrooms where the teacher lectured from the front of the room and students sat silently in rows soaking in knowledge like wordless sponges. Today's classrooms are vastly different. The neat rows have become flexible seating and small group centres. Students are encouraged to interact with the subject and engage in discovery learning. For many students this is a welcome change, for others, however, it can be an overwhelming experience. The IEP takes your child's individual strengths into account. The right accommodations and modifications can illuminate learning for a child who is struggling.

INSTRUCTIONAL STRATEGIES	ASSESSMENT METHODS
Using Task cards/charts/illustrations/large print	Using Text-to-speech technology
Watching a video lesson	Use of a scribe
Providing audiobooks	Completing tests orally
Using anchor charts	Alternative tests (fill in the blank, word banks)
Think Pair Share (Working with others)	Success Criteria Checklists
Using manipulatives	Anecdotal comments or photographs of work

Most students do well with accommodations, modifications or a combination of both. Sometimes, however, *alternative expectations* must be developed for your child. An alternative expectation refers to learning material that is not part of the regular school curriculum. For example; my son's IEP included a section on social skills training because he struggled with the complexities of working cooperatively with others. At recess, the school CYW, or Child and Youth Worker, would pull my son and some of his peers to practise essential social skills like building friendships and maintaining them. School is a very social animal and our children must be able to get along with their peers to maximise learning in the 21st Century classroom.

Gifted students may also be given an IEP to ensure that they are being sufficiently challenged. In this situation, modifications, accommodations or alternative expectations may be required for the student who is doing very well because every student deserves to be challenged.

The IEP has subject pages which list the subjects that your child is taking that require accommodations, modifications, or alternative expectations. Subjects that your child does not need changes for will not be included in the IEP. If your child is struggling with reading but excelling in math, then he or she will have a language page outlining all the modified expectations they will be expected to achieve that term. Any accommodations are listed on a separate page, or tab (in an online copy). Math will not have a subject page because your child is achieving the grade-level expectations already.

For any subject requiring modifications, the IEP must show your child's current level of achievement for that subject and, as mentioned previously, should specify a yearly goal. Curriculum expectations (what your child will learn) will be listed, and all teaching strategies used should appear with each expectation.

Please see the example below for context:

JENNY FOUNTAIN

Birthdate: 2011/01/29   School: Anywhere Public School

OEN: 12345678   Grade: 02

Individual Education Plan

Letter Grade	Current Grade Level	Strand
R	2	READING

Subject Strand: READING

Annual Program Goal

By the end of June 2019, Jenny will recognize and read familiar words with greater fluency.

Term 1/Semester 1

Specific Expectation	Teaching Strategy	Assessment Strategy
• will automatically read 20 pre-primer sight words.	• flashcards • partner pairing • proximity to teacher • assistive technology	• colour cues • alternative setting • extra time

If you would like to see an example of a sample IEP, the Ontario Ministry of Education's document on the IEP is an excellent resource (http://www.edu.gov.on.ca/eng/general/elemsec/speced/guide/resource/iepresguid.pdf).

Transition plans are included on an IEP if your child is 14 and older.[8] The transition plan is intended to help students who may struggle when, moving from one school to another, moving into post-secondary, or transitioning into the work world.

Once again, every staff member who contributes to the creation of your child's IEP will be listed on the document. It will register the staff member's name and their job title. This helps you know who to approach if you have questions about your child's IEP. Once the development process is completed, the school principal will ensure that the IEP is finalized within 30 days (in Ontario). The school principal must see that your child's IEP was completed using his, or her, strengths and needs, that all IPRC recommendations (if any) are included and that the document does include all necessary modifications and/or accommodations. The principal will also check to see that a statement is included about your child's assessments, as well as a date for updating and review of the document.

Put it in Motion!

Once your child's IEP is completed, you will be given a copy to review and sign. The IEP will also be shared with all educators who work with your child, and a copy will be placed in their Ontario Student Record (OSR), or similar file. The educators who work with your child *must* follow the IEP, as it is a legal document. This means that only expectations, accommodations, and modifications listed in the IEP document can be used. It is essential you are knowledgeable with the contents of your child's IEP. When you are discussing your child's day over dinner, if your child is referencing learning expectations that are not part of your child's IEP, do not hesitate to contact your child's teacher. This is especially important during transitions for your child, such as changing grades or moving up to secondary school. I had to have several conversations with high school staff when my son went into grade 9. Many of his accommodations were not being followed by the high school staff. I remember one phone conversation I had with an administrator at his new high school. It was apparent that my son's

IEP was not being followed correctly. When I questioned the administrator, his response was, "Well we do have over 800 students at this school." As an educator, and administrator myself, I was shocked.

Rather than become angry, however, I merely reminded him that the IEP was a legally binding document that needed to be followed. I only share this experience as a cautionary tale. You are your child's best advocate. It is true that most teachers are very conscientious and follow the IEP carefully, but mistakes or miscommunication could occur. If you are concerned about your child's IEP, contact your child's teacher. Education is an equal partnership and works best when we are all on the same page.

Parents and teachers must continually monitor the success, or effectiveness, of the IEP. Your child has a beautiful opportunity to self-advocate here. If your child has reached a certain age, he or she should be aware of his, or her, goals and expectations. If your child understands what he is supposed to be learning, he is more likely to engage in the process. If changes to your child's IEP do need to be made, make sure that your child has been given enough time to work with the expectations before attempting to alter them.

In Ontario, if your child has an IEP with modifications, then the IEP box on the Provincial Report Card must be checked for those subjects where modifications exist. It is not necessary to check the IEP box for accommodations alone.

Check-in

As suggested earlier, because your child's IEP is a working document. The IEP document is always reviewed at the start of a new term, as new expectations are added, and new units are studied. If significant changes are required, your child's school will set up a meeting to go over the changes and the reason for them.

If your child is graduating and going to high school, the elementary school will schedule a transition meeting with the receiving school. At this meeting, educators will discuss your child's strengths, the IEP, and any other relevant factors that could impact a successful transition.

Your child's new school should review the IEP to familiarize themselves with the modifications and accommodations that your child is used to. A new IEP will be developed by the receiving school, and the process begins again at stage one. If your child already has an IEP in place, previous IEP documents will be used as a guide by your child's new school. When my son was in his last year of elementary school, we had several meetings with the high school. It was very reassuring for my son to know that his new teachers had some understanding of his abilities and struggles. He was able to tour the school with the Learning Support Teacher, and this helped relieve his anxiety.

Your child's education is important! The IEP is intended to address your child's unique abilities. We are all of us differently-abled and it is comforting to know that whether your child is gifted, struggles with reading, focus or attention, the IEP is there to keep school staff accountable and your child on track!

"You need to be mindful in education. Everything you do will create a glow, or cast a shadow. You can always become a better teacher, or administrator, as you navigate the years of your career collecting wisdom and experience. Yet most students have only one shot at each grade level. They don't get another chance to impress you. This is likely their only opportunity to get this grade right. See that struggle within them. Always acknowledge their inner spark. If you can do that with most students you will be remembered fondly. But when you can do that consistently, with every student, you will truly live up to the title of teacher."

JENNY FOUNTAIN

SEEING IN THREE DIMENSIONS

SUSAN R. BARRY, PH.D.

Perhaps the most crucial tool for success in school is the ability to read. The role of stable binocular vision in reading is often ignored, and binocular disorders in school children frequently go untreated. As a result, a significant number of children struggle unnecessarily in school. Two groups that should work very closely together are school-teachers and developmental or behavioral optometrists. I learned this the hard way, through my struggles in school.

At first blush, it may seem that good binocular vision is not necessary for reading fluency. After all, you can read with just one eye. However, children with binocular vision disorders, such as strabismus (crossed eyes or walleyes), some types of amblyopia (lazy eye), and convergence insufficiency (see below), are not dealing with the loss of one eye. Their problems arise because, while reading, they do not aim their two eyes at the same location on the page. As a result, input from their two eyes conflicts, resulting in blurred or double vision, or the sensation that the words are moving around on the page. Sadly, these problems are not picked up by the standard school vision screening, which tests only distance vision while viewing with one eye at a time.

These difficulties are all too familiar to me since I suffered from infantile strabismus (crossed eyes from infancy). Although I had three eye muscle surgeries by the time I was seven, I still did not aim the two eyes simultaneously at the same place on the page. Since I was cross-eyed, I cross-fixated. When I was learning to read, my right eye saw letters located to the left of the letters that I saw with my left eye. Although I am not dyslexic, I distinctly remember being in first grade and trying to figure out whether the word I was reading was "saw" or "was." My reading accuracy was poor and reading speed slow. Recent scientific papers on reading in individuals with strabismus or amblyopia document the types of difficulties that I encountered. However, my school principal blamed my reading difficulties on low intelligence and told my mother that she had to face facts — I was a "dim bulb." My mother never forgot those words, nor did she believe them. She taught me how to read when the school gave up on me.

Strabismus occurs in 4% of the population, and amblyopia in 3 %. Even more common, however, is convergence insufficiency, found in at least 8 % of individuals. This disorder is not often recognized because the child's eyes generally appear straight. Indeed, the child may align the eyes properly for binocular vision while looking in the distance. While looking at a near target, however, such as words on a page or computer screen, one eye fixates the letters while the other wanders outward. Although the words may appear double or blurry or may appear to move on the page, the child, knowing no other way of seeing, does not realize that these views are abnormal and indicative of a vision problem.

Reading is an endurance activity. Although a child with a binocular disorder may read a single line or paragraph without too much difficulty, the added effort in aiming the eyes together at the same word on the page, or in interpreting confusing images from misaligned eyes, builds up over minutes. We would never expect a child with a limp to run on the playground as far or as fast as a child who walks normally. When evaluating a child's academic progress, however, we generally ignore their ability to sustain coordination of their eyes for near viewing. Given the frequency of binocular vision disorders, at least one to two children in a class of twenty may encounter reading problems as a result of binocular deficits.

Binocular disorders can be treated effectively with optometric vision therapy, usually provided by a developmental or behavioral optometrist. Indeed, a 2008 National Eye Institute study of 221 children demonstrated that a combination of home and office vision therapy was the most effective treatment for convergence insufficiency. Further studies indicate that treatment of convergence insufficiency reduces academic problems.

Thus, reading difficulties in many children could be reduced or eliminated with proper diagnosis and treatment of binocular vision problems.

Although I had been cross-eyed since infancy, I did not consult a developmental optometrist until I was 48 years old because, like most of the population, I was not aware of their work. The optometrist prescribed a program of optometric vision therapy that taught me how to aim both eyes simultaneously at the same spatial location. As a result, I learned to see stereoscopically for the first time and can now read more quickly and easily. Indeed, the changes were so transformative that I wrote a book about binocular vision, binocular disorders, and the science behind optometric vision therapy titled *Fixing My Gaze: A Scientist's Journey into Seeing in Three Dimensions*. The book was endorsed by two Nobel laureates in neuroscience (Dr.'s Eric Kandel and David Hubel), received excellent reviews in *The New England Journal of Medicine* and *Nature Neuroscience*, has been translated into six languages, and was rated the fourth-best science book of 2009 by the editors of Amazon.com. What's more, I have received more than 1.000 emails, specifically from individuals with binocular disorders seeking treatment for their condition. Clearly, my story has touched a nerve.

"The key to the future of the world is finding the optimistic stories and letting them be known."

PETE SEEGER, AMERICAN SONGWRITER AND FOLKSINGER

CONCLUSION

If you see issues in any of the five areas (see Empowering Parents and Educators chapter), then get a more in-depth assessment for your child. Visit www.covd.org to find a USA FCOVD Board Certified Eye Doctor for a full VSA workup. Use the "Locate A Doctor" tool, click the "Board Certified in Vision Therapy" box below your information and fill in "Advanced Search Options." This is so that you can find eye doctors who are (USA) Board Certified in Optometric Vision Therapy. The initials "FCOVD" after the doctor's name stands for "Fellow of the College of Optometrists in Vision Development." This designation means that the eye doctor in question has completed rigorous training and examinations in the field of Optometric Vision Therapy.

Let me add a bit of professional history to the story.

The Optometric Extension Foundation (OEP) was founded in 1928 by Dr. A.M. Skeffington. The goal of the foundation was to educate optometrists concerning concepts that Skeffington had developed.

Dr. Skeffington, known as the Father of Behavioral Optometry, graduated from the Needles Institute and practiced in Kearney, Nebraska before devoting himself to the OEP until his death.

He had observed that many of his patients would have symptoms that appeared visual, but upon examination, would not show traditional visual dysfunctions. Additionally, he noticed that many individuals in this group struggled with near activities. He hypothesized that socially compulsive near activities (reading, etc.) caused stress that interfered with the effortless functioning of the eyes since the eyes were not meant to be used for prolonged periods of detailed near work such as reading. This increased stress caused an innervational mismatch between two effector systems of the eyes.

Dr. Skeffington reasoned that vision, as opposed to eyesight was a product of four sub-systems. The first system is what he termed anti-gravity (proprioceptive/kinesthetic, labyrinthine and ocular) that oriented the body in space; the second the centering system that located the object in space; the third the identification system that gleaned useful information about the object and the environment. The fourth and last aspect was the speech-auditory system that allowed the person to describe what has been seen and also to reverse the process to be able to hear/read and "see" what someone else had described.

SKEFFINGTON'S FOUR CIRCLES

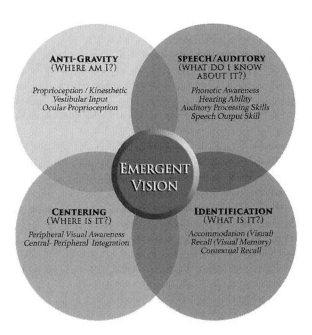

The College of Optometrists in Vision Development (COVD) is an international board certifying organization that certifies optometrists who generally practice following the teachings of Skeffington.

He untiringly devoted himself to society by constantly striving to improve vision care that he and other colleagues in the profession developed at the time. The profession owes him a debt of gratitude.

It should be kept in mind, however, that although COVD is an international organization, the FCOVD designation is mainly an American based designation, in terms of being formally recognized by regulatory bodies as an advanced competency designation. In time, we hope that all optometric regulatory bodies worldwide will recognize this designation as an important specialty in the field of optometric care.

Searching the COVD website, you will quickly see that there are FCOVDs in many countries around the world. You can be referred to an FCOVD doctor by your regular family eye doctor , or you can also call an office directly to schedule a consult. In our clinic network, for example, when patients or parents call for an appointment, they are told that we do not offer *routine eye exams*. This is due to the complex nature of optometric vision therapy and rehabilitation. We dedicate 100% of our clinical efforts and research* goals solely towards the area of optometric vision therapy.

In my story, I am living my dream of marrying academic research to clinical care. We not only treat patients but we also track their data and constantly look for ways to refine and improve the therapy process, using the outcome data as a guide. In the words of Einstein, "I have no special talents. I am only passionately curious." We understand the equations are one thing, but the people behind the equations are what drive us.

I think my mother would be proud to see my dream become a reality. This is also thanks, in no small part; to the great people I have around me at our VUE³ Vision Therapy Clinics (www.vuetherapy.ca.) Watching how they care for our patients is an inspiration to me every day. The inspiring Vision and Mission statement for our group was developed by our team. They are indeed the heroes in the trenches

---

* Our research only uses the treatment data collected with the patient's informed written consent.

with me. I love my team!

Our Vision Statement:

Empower people and unlock human potential.
Our Mission Statement:

Embrace and drive change through the passionate application of clinical research, using Optometric Vision Therapy, to remove the stigma of failure by enhancing natural curiosity.

I am now surrounded by several colleagues doing work with a powerful "WHY " factor. We love what we do, and we KNOW that we make a difference. We are quite simply blessed. It may sound odd, but I thank God every day for the blessing of the issues I endured in the past. They ultimately led to my life today. Looking at my daughter, who is in grade 1, yet reading at a grade 3 level, I would not change a thing. This journey has taught me humility as a doctor, patience as a parent, and empathy as a person. It has also ingrained in me the constant need to ask, "Why " and to never give up in the battle to help our children.

Thank you for taking the time to read this book. I hope you feel supported as a parent, teacher, or other professional caring for children with academic struggles.

Be inspired to action, ask questions!

Be a hero in your child's life!

"Two roads diverged in a wood, and I—I took the one less traveled by, And that has made all the difference."

ROBERT FROST

AFTERWORDS

DR. DANIEL J. CUNNINGHAM, O.D., FCOVD

"It" always begins with a question in search of an answer. What "it" is can be described as a thirst for knowledge, or, a resolution to a problem. Sometimes, "it" is merely the avoidance of unpleasant experiences. Whatever "it" is that drove you to pick up this book, I hope that Dr. Quaid's story resonates with you. Maybe your child is struggling in school, and you have seen countless professionals and done too many therapies to care to list. Perhaps you were the struggling student, but you worked hard and made a good life for you. Or maybe you didn't. It doesn't matter, you're here now, and you read this book in search of answers.

We do not pretend that Optometric Vision Therapy is the be-all and end-all to every reading problem. Teachers, tutors, speech-language pathologists, occupational therapists, and countless other professionals are vital to helping the child that struggles to read overcome their barriers. However, the definition of vision that Dr. Quaid talks about in this book is often overlooked. By now, that point should be clear. Just like Dr. Quaid, I've had countless parents ask me why more eye care professionals do not know more about this area. I have no easy answer for them. For some, it is that their schooling did not teach them about it. For others, they found no interest in this area of vision care. For others yet, it is just easier to ignore it. There are probably dozens of reasons, but for the parent and the child that made it to my exam room; all that matters is that there is hope and relief. Hope that this doctor actually has the answers and relief that there may be an end to the struggle.

Vision is so complex that it is often difficult to simplify the message. Dr. Quaid's personal journey, shared with you in this book, lit the fire that is at the root of his motivation for getting the "message to the masses" about vision, the negative impacts that poor vision can have and (here's the best part) that something can be done to affect positive change. Optometric vision therapy can, and does, remove the shackles to efficient learning and living! Dr. Quaid has an insatiable desire to tell anyone who will listen about what vision really is (Hint: It is way more than 20/20, if you have not already been told that enough times).

My personal journey with vision therapy began while in Optometry school. I had never heard of vision therapy (sound familiar?) before that point. We had classes and labs that taught us about various conditions, their diagnoses, and treatments, but what really caught my attention was a lecture by one of the local optometrists on the real-life benefits of vision therapy. In my second year of optometry school, Dr. Rick Morris lectured to us one afternoon about dozens of examples of children who were struggling in school, and through optometric vision therapy, were able to become successful, not just in school, but in sports and in life in general! While Dr. Morris stood and lectured to my class of 106 optometry students, my enthusiasm toward learning more about vision therapy grew and grew. I had such a draw to Dr. Morris' lecture that I am pretty sure I had to pick my jaw up off my desk literally. I looked around the lecture hall expecting to see everyone as engaged as I was with Dr. Morris' lecture. That is not my memory of that day. Instead of 106 highly engaged future optometrists, I saw apathy around the room. I liken the situation to the high school student that might ask, "When will I ever use algebra in real life?" Of those 106 students, I know that I am the only one of my classmates that is Board Certified (FCOVD) in vision therapy, and most likely, the only one utilizing optometric vision therapy. That may seem like a bleak future for optometric vision therapy and the masses of people that need access to vision therapy. But worry not, with optometrists like Dr. Quaid and his experience sitting on the Board of Directors at the College of Optometrists in Vision Development (COVD), the message is getting out. Dr. Quaid often reports back on the overwhelming enthusiasm that the graduating classes of optometrists have for vision therapy. In my home province of Ontario and across Canada, there has been an explosion of optometrists providing vision therapy. The future is truly bright!

I first met Dr. Quaid in 2007, when I spent six months working with him at IRIS The Visual Group in Guelph, Ontario. I would again join Dr. Quaid in practicing optometry in 2014, and continue to this day when he asked me to join his vision therapy practice. I am not exactly sure what ultimately led to Dr. Quaid and I striking up a friendship out that initial short work relationship. I believe that it is due to our shared thirst for knowledge, always asking, "Why?" I could take up pages telling you about the many "why" questions that Dr. Quaid and I ask pertaining to vision. I'll spare you that burden. Just know that we have special "blue-sky" thinking time on a regular basis that allows us to appease our thirst for "why." "Why" is a great question, but if you never ask follow-up questions like "What" and "How," you will never affect much change to anyone. This is where Dr. Quaid really shines. I often refer to Dr. Quaid as my "personal Pub Med" for his uncanny ability to know every single research article ever written about vision therapy (or a least it seems that way). He also has an insatiable desire to add to the volumes of research that already exist on vision therapy, and by doing so, we are striving for each patient to reach their maximum potential, or as our "vision statement" at VUE[3] Vision Therapy states: "To empower people and unlock human potential."

Our purpose through vision therapy is to act as a guide to the patient on their journey to removing the shackles of dysfunctional vision. We strive to help you understand "it" and equip you with tools and experiences so that you, or your child, may harness visions' full power. My hope for you is that after having read this book, you will be better empowered to ask the questions that you need to, in order to find your answers to "it."

STEPHANIE BEAUDETTE

I was the kid that fell through the cracks in the school system. I did not excel, and I did not misbehave. My parents would help me study and try their hardest to help me succeed in school, but I just didn't understand certain subjects. I chose to make people believe that I just didn't try, "if I wanted to do well I could, but I just didn't try."

It was my coping mechanism because I didn't want anyone to know I was struggling. I was supposed to understand this and I didn't, so I must be a failure. As I grew towards adulthood, I chose to only do activities that I knew I could succeed at and would avoid doing things that I knew would put me into a stressful or vulnerable state. The reality is that I didn't have all the visual skills required to learn so I couldn't process information as well as other kids. I know if my parents had known about Vision Therapy and how it could have helped me, they would have signed me up, but the knowledge wasn't common while I was a child and teenager.

After I met Dr. Quaid in 2012 and found out about Vision Therapy I knew I had to work with him and try to help educate as many people as possible about how Vision Therapy can change lives.

When I started working with Dr. Quaid, my job was to help the patients when they left his exam room; I can't count how many parents cried when they left his office. They were a mixed of tears. The tears of happiness for finally discovering why their child has been struggling blended with tears of guilt for either not believing their child, or not finding the answer sooner. My role was to make sure they understood the logistics of Vision Therapy, to book them in the schedule. We had limited availability at first with only one Vision Therapist, and it was amazing to see the level of commitment people would be willing to invest in improving the lives of their children. In so many cases people would be traveling significant distances (often will over 1.5 hours of highway driving) to get to our facility, but they didn't hesitate to take mid-day appointment if it was the only opening in the schedule because their child's future was that important to them.

Throughout the therapy sessions, there are follow up appointments with Dr. Quaid to review the progress and results and while people still came out of Dr. Quaid's office crying, they were now usually tears of joy! The results showed that their child was improving and at home. It was usually seen since homework was no longer the battle it once was, fewer complaints of headaches, and the child was less disruptive in school. This young person was gaining confidence. They could read a book by themselves. These are activities that we often take for granted as part of day-to-day life but for a child who is struggling, or a parent who has watched their child struggle, overcoming these challenges are life-changing.

In 2014, Dr. Quaid opened a facility dedicated to Vision Therapy, we had two Vision Therapists when we opened and by the end of the year had a team of five Vision Therapists. The company has grown over the years, but the mission has always been the same, empower people, and unlock human potential by using vision therapy to remove the negative stigma of failure. Our ultimate goal is to promote vision therapy and graduate as many patients as possible, something we strive for every day and try to instill in our team. Today I have less interaction with the patients; my role has evolved to help create the systems to make the practice run smoothly and support our team. I want every patient who walks into our clinic to have an amazing experience. We dedicate a lot of time to reviewing our operations to generate positive results for our patients. I love talking with patients and their families about their experiences and asking them how we can make the process better for them. In my years of working in this field, what I have learned is that managing patient expectations is vital.

Vision Therapy can change your life, but it takes time, work, and dedication to achieve positive results. As with any therapy, you get out of it what you put into it. Dr. Cunningham is an advocate that we don't change the patient, the patient changes themselves; we just show them how to do it and that positive change is possible. Vision Therapy is a commitment, and there may be barriers to signing up, for some it is distance, for some it's money, for some it's time and for some it's all three. Every family has to evaluate their life and determine if Vision Therapy is something they can commit to and make a priority, if it's not right now, that's okay. It is better to wait until you can commit to it as a family than to start and have to stop mid-way because you couldn't do the drive, spend the time, or afford it right now.

If you do sign up for a Vision Therapy program, my best advice is make sure you attend all your in office appointments and to do the home activities as much or as little as your Vision Therapist or Optometrist recommend. We understand that life happens and sometimes an appointment needs to be missed, or homework doesn't get done. That's okay, but try to schedule a make-up session and get back on the homework band-wagon next week. I do all the clinical statistics[*] and what I've found is that the more consistent patients are with their in office sessions and homework, the faster we see results. Always be honest with your therapy team, listen, ask questions and always do your best.

*"If you want to go fast, go alone.
If you want to go far, go together".*

AUTHOR UNKNOWN

---

[*]   Our research only uses the treatment data collected with the patient's informed written consent.

APPENDIX

Struggling Students: A Global Problem

Millions of parents search for answers to their children's learning difficulties. "There is a light at the end of the tunnel," says Dr. David Damari, Past President of the College of Optometrists in Vision Development (COVD). "Statistically, more than 60% of children who struggle with reading have underlying vision problems contributing to their challenges."

But it is not the type of vision problem most people imagine. Most of the children who have vision problems that interfere with reading and learning can see the letters on the eye chart just fine. So when parents told their children had passed a vision screening, what they are being told is that their child can see the letters on the eye chart from a distance of 20 feet (6 meters.) The problem lies in what was not tested. How well do the two eyes work together when reading? How do they move on the page or track a line of print? These are just a few of the 17 visual skills required for academic success.

It does not matter what the curriculum is or even in what country you live. When children have underlying vision problems contributing to their learning challenges, they continue to struggle until the vision problem is corrected.

Michael Prolman shared about his 9-year-old daughter. "My wife would say, 'You can see the steam come out of her ears when Serena struggled to read at home.' We could not understand why such a highly intelligent girl, with a vocabulary many years ahead of her age, had so much trouble reading. In the second grade, her frustration grew to the point where she no longer wanted to read."

Fortunately, a psychologist referred them to a developmental optometrist who opened the door to a solution. Serena had convergence insufficiency, which is a very treatable eye coordination disorder that can make reading very difficult. Convergence insufficiency is treated by optometric vision therapy.

After vision therapy, "Serena now reads one year ahead of her grade level. Recently, Serena invited me to read alongside her on the sofa. While she was reading her book, I occasionally looked surreptitiously over the top of mine, to observe her completely absorbed in a world of words. It was one of the most deeply satisfying moments I have experienced as a parent."

Even in Malaysia, parents are dealing with the same problems. Tim Lim had low self-esteem and also thought he was stupid. The Dyslexia Association Malaysia referred Tim Lim to a developmental optometrist in Kuala Lumpur who was able to get to the root of the problem. Tim Lim had convergence insufficiency. Once the vision problem was corrected his mother, Ang Si Ying, saw a huge difference. "Now Tim Lim is starting to use his brain, and he is very intelligent! He no longer throws tantrums when asked to do schoolwork, and homework gets done much faster."

Andreas Lizardos from Greece had to wait until he was an adult to get help. When he was in school, he had difficulty focusing and had trouble understanding the lesson. Even as an adult, he would get nervous and confused when his work required him to read for more than one hour either in print or on the computer. After optometric vision therapy, "I have noticed remarkable improvement. I can focus for extended periods without any problem. I strongly recommend this therapy to all that have similar problems, especially for children."

For more information, or to find a doctor near you, please visit covd.org.

Dr. David Damari is the Past President of COVD and the Association of Schools and Colleges of Optometry

Below are some linked articles for further reading. Please visit the COVD website:

www.covd.org/page/Press_Releases

2016 Sports-Related Concussion

01/18/16 Concussion: Parents Speak Out about the Visual Link to Recovery

2015 Learning Disabilities Awareness Month

09/28/15 Inadequate Vision Screenings Contributing to Epidemic of Children with Learning Problems

2015 August is International Children's Vision & Learning Month

08/04/15 Eye Coordination Problems Can Make Words "Hop Like Frogs"

07/02/15 Optometrists focus on Visual Symptoms from Concussions that Block Learning

06/04/15 Texas Mother Shares How She Put an End to Homework Battles

2015 Autism Awareness Month

04/01/15 Helping Children with Autism Focus on the World Around Them

2015 Brain Injury Awareness Month

03/02/15 Missing Link to the Rehabilitation Process

2014 August is International Children's Vision & Learning Month

10/01/14 Vision Problems Masquerade as Learning Disabilities

08/19/14 Critical Link between Vision and Learning

08/04/14 Could Your Child's Struggle with Reading and Learning be Due to an Undiagnosed Vision Problem?

07/01/14 Learning Problems Can Be in the Eyes: A Back-to-School Message

06/05/14 Poor Grades Explained by Vision Problems

05/09/14 Childhood Reading Struggles: The Answer may be in the Eyes.

2014 Autism Awareness Month

04/09/14 A Missing Piece to the Autism Puzzle

2014 Brain Injury Awareness Month

03/03/14 Help for Double Vision

2013 August is International Children's Vision & Learning Month

10/01/13 Vision Problems Mistaken for Learning Disabilities

08/20/13 Grandmother Finally Learns How to Read: "Never Give Up"

08/01/13 COVD Joins with Author, Educator, & Expert in Early Learning Success, Dr. Bob Sornson in Saying "It's Time to Stop Arguing and Help Our Children!!"

07/08/13 Struggling Students: A Global Problem with a Universal Solution

06/03/13 Missing Link to Common Core State Standards

2013 Autism Awareness Month

04/01/13 Signs of Autism: PSA Provides Parents with a New Look

2012 August is National Children's Vision & Learning Month

07/10/12 Mom of Struggling Reader Finds Help and Speaks Out

06/04/12 Spread the Word About the Critical Link Between Vision & Learning

05/09/12 Visual Skills Necessary for Reading and Learning

2011 August is National Children's Vision & Learning Month

09/20/11 Visions of Hope Winner Announced

08/01/11 Mom & Daughter offer Advice to Parents for Back-to-School

07/18/11 What It Can Mean When Your Child Says "I'm Stupid"

06/06/11 Educators Find New Hope for Struggling Students

05/02/11 Hidden Roadblocks: What Parents Need To Know About Vision and Learning

2010 August is National Children's Vision & Learning Month

07/08/10 Vision, Learning & Dyslexia - All-Pro Arizona Cardinals Wide Receiver Larry Fitzgerald Sets the Record Straight

07/26/10 Don't Leave Your Child's Vision Behind - All-Pro Arizona Cardinals' Wide Receiver Larry Fitzgerald Celebrates 'August is National Children's Vision and Learning Month'

08/04/10 Most Back to School Shopping Lists Are Missing 17 Critical Items - Doctors offer advice to parents to ensure academic success

2005-2009 Press Releases

04/14/05 Poor Performance on Standardized Tests Can Signal a Vision Problem According to the College of Optometrists in Vision Development

07/08/05 Parents Need to Focus on Vision as Key to Learning

2008 "August Is Children's Vision And Learning Month" Public Awareness Campaign Launched by the College Of Optometrists In Vision Development (COVD)

10/14/08 New Research Gives Hope to Children With Common Reading-Related Vision Disorder

07/18/09 Arizona Cardinals' Wide-Receiver and Pro Bowl MVP, Larry Fitzgerald Encourages Parents to Take Action TODAY

9/29/09 NAACP Passes Resolution on Optometric Vision Therapy

10/01/09 NAACP Endorses Optometric Vision Therapy at its 100th anniversary Convention

ENDNOTES

ADHD – Diagnosis or Symptom?

Even basic uncorrected long-sightedness, which means a person has a "+" prescription in their glasses, (you can tell as the lenses make things bigger), is a risk factor for ADHD. Research has shown that after using drops called Cycloplegic Drops if a child's prescription is higher than +2 units, problems may be induced to tick enough boxes in ADHD questions to trigger a diagnosis. Many dilating drops are primarily used to enlarge the pupil, but some have a side effect of cycloplegia, giving the patient the typical temporary blurry vision at near after an eye exam. Reading issues are likely to start manifesting if there are more than +2.00 units. Left uncorrected, there is sufficient strain to trigger enough symptoms on the Connors Rating Scale (CRS), to trigger a diagnosis of ADHD. This is not a high prescription. This also assumes that the eye-teaming and oculomotor systems are intact, which may not be the case.

There are subtle changes from the older DSM-IV (Diagnostic and Statistical Manual of Mental Disorders) to the newer DSM-V manual, which is a list of required symptoms one must have to be diagnosed with a psychiatric disorder. Many parents do not realize that ADHD is considered to be under this category.

An interesting addition was put in the newer version (DSM-V). It states that the symptoms (enough checked boxes apply), allow someone to be diagnosed, but only in the absence of other neurosensory disorders. However, the DSM-V does not specifically state this in these words. What the DSM-V does say, is that the symptoms have to be persistent regardless of the environment.

Therefore, according to the DSM-V, if for example reading based symptoms that are more obvious at school (i.e. less obvious during summer or at weekends) which cause attentional issues at school, which is often the pattern in children with poor eye co-ordination skills, should not be considered for an ADHD diagnosis. For example, we often hear from parents that "Our child does not need the medication during the summer." This observation should in fact be an alarm bell. After all, a requirement for ADHD diagnosis is that the symptoms are there under most if not all circumstances, regardless of the environment. Visual issues typically show much more issues with reading and/or schooling environments.

I believe that a visual issue such as Convergence Insufficiency, which is indeed a neuro-sensory disorder, would apply here. Some may say that CI is a muscle issue and not a sensory issue, as the eyes are the problem but, with all due respect, I would disagree.

In CI, the eyes function almost perfectly ONE EYE AT A TIME. The issue is that they do not *team together* as they should. So, if the eyes are fine monocularly but not when they have to work together, this is not an eye issue. More specifically, CI is a problem with how the brain processes (or in this case does not process) and merges the visual information from each eye. CI in fact has little to do with the actual musculature itself in terms of causation. The brain has difficulty controlling the fusional apparatus appropriately. In essence, the issue may manifest at the eye-teaming level, but make no mistake; it is a brain issue at the end of the day. If at least 40% of the primate brain is visual machinery, then I believe an eye-teaming issue should qualify as a "neuro-sensory disorder". Therefore, according to the DSM-V, eye-teaming issues such as CI should be tested for and treated thoroughly, before considering a default diagnosis of ADHD. In my clinical experience, this is ever hardly done, even though research indicates it should be done, especially in cases of suspected ADHD.

Starting the Journey of Vision Assessment

If you are a research-minded individual, as many of my patients are, you can reference out a publication on this topic. Just go to www. pubmed.com and search my name (Quaid P) and look for the 2013 paper we published in a journal called, Graefes Archives of Clinical & Experimental Ophthalmology. This paper outlines most of the tests that I will briefly describe here but in more detail. It also lists many references to other peer-reviewed journals. All this concludes that children with reading-based learning difficulties should have this more detailed work-up of their visual skills. It is essential to note that this paper had to be vetted by several ophthalmologists, and they came to agree with us after a thorough review of the research data.

After the routine eye examination, with or without issues raised and if a child continues to have reading issues, where a symptom score on the CITT questionnaire was indeed >15/60, what should this more in-depth Visual Skills Assessment (VSA) look like?

In our clinic, it is a two-step process. Each appointment is usually about 1.5 hours (as opposed to the routine eye examination, which is generally in the range of 20-30mins). The first step is called a "VIP" assessment, Visual Information Processing assessment, and consists of mainly visual processing test batteries.

I have listed the tests we use in our clinic and a brief description of what is being tested in the table below. You can see that this is not a typical eye testing battery. We are looking at more in-depth issues, like visual memory, reading efficacy and tracking skills, for example. We are looking not at the mechanics of the eye as such, but looking more at what the brain does with the information sent by the eyes. The VIP assessment looks at the visual software and whether it is working properly. These results are measured in percentiles for the most part.

In explaining a percentile, it is entirely different than a percentage. If one scores 50% on a test, that is typically a bad result. However, if I score in the 50th percentile, it means I am bang on average (i.e., out of 100 people my age, I scored better than half of them, and half of them scored better than me).

Typically, any score under the 37th percentile is a concern, and any score under the 25th percentile is definitely a concern. So, for example, if I score in the 12th percentile, this means that out of 100 people my age, I ranked 12th from the bottom of the list.

VIP Test Names TVPS = Test of Visual Processing Skills	Every day life example (i.e. what would be noted by parent or teacher if area deficient?)
TVPS: Visual Discrimination Skills test	Substitutions when reading (i.e. saying something similar to what is on the page but not exactly what is on the page – i.e. kitchen for kitten).
TVPS: Visual Memory (VM) Skills test	Child cannot recall what a word looks like despite seeing it several times, usually ends up spelling it "how it sounds" (i.e. future, as "fucher").
TVPS: Spatial Relations Visual Skills test	Orientation skills (i.e. can the child rotate an image in their head and predict what it would look like a different way round?). Linked to reversal tendencies and copying / transposing numbers (i.e. 23 as 32, or 15 as 51).
TVPS: Visual Closure Visual Skills test	The ability to predict what the "big picture is" from seeing an image of it "half completed".
TVPS: Figure-Ground Visual Skills test	Difficulty ignoring background information (i.e., gets overwhelmed with extra print on page and must cover up the print not being read, to cope with the busy visual information. Gets lost in the details when reading.
TVPS: Form Constancy Visual Skills test	Ability to see the same object or shape, even when it appears in a different orientation or size. Misreads words, guesses at words and shows reversal tendencies on written output. Think about the mirror neuron conversation elsewhere in the book!

VIP Test Names TVPS = Test of Visual Processing Skills	Every day life example (i.e. what would be noted by parent or teacher if area deficient?)
TVPS: Sequential VM Visual Skills test	Ability to remember a certain sequence of shapes (different to regular VM as this is more "gestalt" testing.) Shows if the child is visually remembering or using auditory to recall sequence of shapes (i.e. do I just look at it or do I tend to say the sequence to myself? If this score is low, the child will likely struggle with spelling issues, phonetic approach and formula recall in mathematics.
DEM testing: H & V Tracking	Tracking test, if results are low, the child will need to use a ruler or their finger, to help them not lose their place when reading.
TOSWRF-2 test: *Reading Efficiency test*	Assesses how quickly the child can decode and recognize words. The test is a very good predictor of reading performance in the classroom. If result is low, this tends to go hand in hand with low sequential VM and horizontal DEM tracking scores in particular.
WOLD test: Sentence Copying Test	Assesses how quickly a child can copy 29 words from one page to another. If low, child has issues copying information quickly in school from the board to a page, usually related to visual memory issues and low DEM score.
Piaget Laterality and Gardiner Reversal test:	Assesses the tendency of a child to comprehend their left from right. Also assesses age appropriate tendencies in terms of letter and/or number reversals. If result is low, reversals on written output tend to be common, as well as mixing up b's with d's and p's with q's in lower case letter use.

This VIP testing is done with the current habitual or normal ocular status. In other words, they wear glasses if they already have them and wear no glasses if they don't. We assess them *as they present* to us.

The data attained is called the Baseline VIP Data and is vital, as it will be used to compare subsequent Checkpoint Data, to determine if we are making gains in therapy.

Now, the reason we re-assess the data every 12 sessions (at a frequency of one session per week) or the equivalent of 3 months is to avoid any learning effect. In other words, if we test the patient too frequently, they may get better scores, simply because they are memorizing the test. This would not show valid results of actual gains from the therapy. Also, we change the templates on some of the tests, to further reduce this possible learning effect.

Some of the VIP tests we use are timed, while others have no timing component to them at all. This is important in the testing process, as some children do better when they not under time pressure. These kids may fall apart, so to speak, when they have to do a visual task quickly. These are typically the children that have, "Extra time required." or "Need extra time to copy information from the board to the page." specifically stated in their IEP.

Once the VIP assessment is done, we typically bring the patient back on a different day, (to avoid fatigue), to do the oculomotor testing. The oculomotor testing component is referred to as a Visual Skills Assessment (VSA). So, to be more exact in my terminology, the total assessment consists of a VIP assessment, followed by a VSA assessment, each component being about 1.5 hours each, totaling 3 hours of complete, thorough testing.

The VSA aspect is vital for a few reasons. Firstly, it allows us to look for patterns in the data, from a hardware standpoint, that may explain patterns found with the software, VIP assessment. We typically find that specific patterns of VIP data go hand-in-hand, with certain patterns of VSA findings. For example, if the DEM (tracking) testing in the VIP component shows poor horizontal tracking and fairly standard vertical tracking, this usually corresponds to a poor NPC result (i.e., the child has a hard time pulling the eyes inwards towards the nose, as in reading).

Doctors in effect are akin to medical detectives trying to solve a case. Using clues (VIP findings), and apparent functional problems (VSA findings), our job is to map one to the other and create an effective plan for how we can fix the functional issues, to then hopefully eliminate the VIP issues. Patients come to us stating, "I see double. My reading is not good." or "I get tired very quickly when I read." They come to us with VIP symptoms. At the clinic, our team must find the underlying *cause* of these symptoms and strive to resolve those issues. Detection is tricky enough, but the real challenge is fixing the problems.

There is an exhaustive list of VSA tests from which to gather data. Here are some we use most commonly in our office.

1. Functionally Based Case History: This is very detailed, asking questions about birth history, prematurity, birth weight, developmental milestones (i.e., when did they walk?), any history of concussions, issues watching 3D, motion sickness history, the pattern of phonetic spelling, etc.
2. Accommodative Facility (+/-2DS testing): This testing, called MAF or Monocular Accommodative Facility, involves a +2DS lens and a -2DS lens. One lens makes your eye relax its focus, while the other makes your eye pull things into focus. While one eye is occluded (covered), the lenses are placed alternating over the eye, between the +/- sides. The child has to report whether the print becomes clear or stays blurry while looking through the lens.

A normal result for a child under 20 years old should be about 12 cycles per minute. This means their focus can change from the plus side to the minus side 24 times in 60 seconds. The test is then performed on the other eye, and a comparison is made. If the eyes are not equal or are very different, it is an indication that the patient will show symptoms, like fatigue, when working closely with print. They will have issues switching their visual system from distance to near and vice versa. This test will record data for the right eye (OD) and the left eye (OS), respectively.

Accommodative Facility testing can also be done with both eyes together, BAF or Binocular Accommodative Facility, with a similar normative value expected. BAF testing measures how the eyes combine binocular eye-teaming skills and monocular near-far focusing skills. It does not test exactly the same thing as MAF, which tests one eye at a time. Interestingly enough, one can, pass the MAF test in each eye separately but fail the BAF testing. This means that the brain has a hard time combining monocular and binocular visual information and lacks "flexibility."

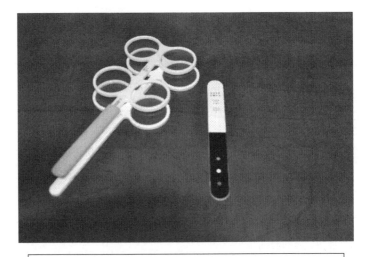

Flipper used for MAF/RAF testing with a standard near point fixation stick with both letters and dots (reverse side has pictures for children.) The test is typically done with 20/30 print at near.

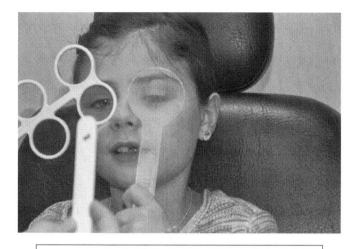

MAF testing with =/-2DS lenses of the right eye.
Note that the occluder blocks the left eye enough so that it is not
included but the doctor can still see how both eyes move.

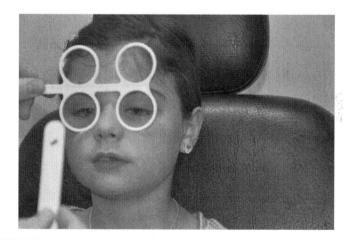

BAF

IMAGES OF FLIPPERS (+/-2DS flippers) BEING USED ON A PATIENT
MONOCULARLY AND BINOCULARLY

BAF testing with +/-2DS lenses with both eyes. This test looks at both monocular
near far focussing skills and convergence and divergence *combined* and is a much
higher level test as both systems have to be intact to pass this test

The doctor can also look at the pupils of the child which will con-tract (i.e., get smaller) as they look closer and closer to the text. When the limit of accommodation is reached, typically the pupil can also be *SEEN* to dilate somewhat. Therefore, there is a nice objective confirm-ation of what would otherwise be a subjective test.

3. Amplitudes of Accommodation (AoA): This test involves moving a standard size of print towards the eye, initially one eye at a time and then both eyes together until the patient can no longer see the letters clearly. The distance of the text from the eye is then recorded and converted to Dioptres, a unit of measurement used to quantify the focussing effort. Easily calculated, a dioptre is measured using centimeters, converted into meters and then by inverting the fraction to arrive at the dioptres measurement.

An example would be, a patient looking at standard (20/30) print at near. As the print is brought closer to the eyes, they can see clearly until the paper is 10cm away. At this point, the print goes consistently blurry. Given that 10cm = 0.1m, we take 0.1m as a decimal and change it into its equivalent fraction of 1/10. Then by inverting that fraction, you arrive at the measurement of 10 dioptres. Therefore, focusing print to 10cm from the eye for this patient requires 10 "dioptres" of focusing effort.

This important measurement can then be compared to a Norma-tive Data Formula that indicates if the AoA is low or abnormal. This formula is 18.5, subtract a third of the patient's age. So for example, if the patient is 15 years old, they should have a measurement of 18.5 subtract 5, (a third of 15), giving the patient a measurement of 13.5 dioptres of focusing ability. If the patient's actual measure of mon-ocular AoA is 20cm, meaning they can clear text at a distance of 20cm from the nose, this is an issue. In the formula, 20cm = 0.2m. This is 2/10 as a fraction. The fraction is simplified to 1/5, which when in-verted is 5. This means that at 15 years old if the patient has only five dioptres of focusing ability and the normative value for this person should at least be 13.5 units, there is indeed a problem.

If a patient is more than 3-4 units below the average value, then usually this indicates a problem with the internal focusing mechanisms of the eye. As a side note, for those of us over 45 years old, you will understand this issue when your "arms are not long enough anymore" to read. This is normal for those over 40 years of age to have this issue, but most certainly is not normal for children.

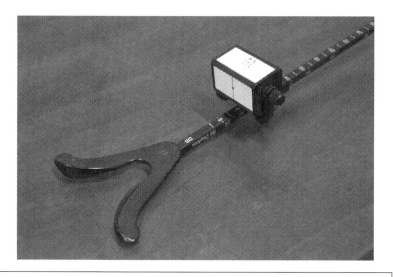

RAF Rule
Measuring device for amplitudes of accomodation and other OM tests that conveniently has all the scales so the doctor does not have to do the conversions between cm and dioptres "on the fly". The "feet-like" end rests on the cheeks of the patient. The drum can be rotated to also use the line which can also be used to measure near point convergence. (NPC)

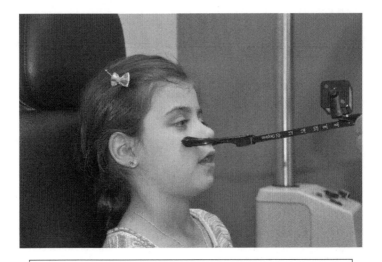

Image of the RAF rule to measure binocular amplitudes of accommodation

4. Horizontal and Vertical Vergence Ranges: The term Vergence Range, is used to describe how much strain the binocular eye-teaming system can handle before it gives out. With this test, we prefer to use a prism bar, which puts an increasing load of strain on the fusional system of the eyes as a team. We then increase the load on the eyes, until they give out in effect, and see two of everything or double. It is akin to a stress test of the eye alignment system.

We do this test, in this manner, at a distance and at near, as well as on the horizontal fusional system and the vertical fusional system. It is important that the inward eye tolerance is about twice the outward eye tolerance. This makes sense, as we turn the eyes "inwards" towards the nose, much more than "outwards" in day-to-day life. Therefore the converging system (the ability to pull the eyes inward), should be more robust, compared to the diverging system (the ability to pull the eyes outward). Normative data does exist for this information, as shown in our published 2013 paper.

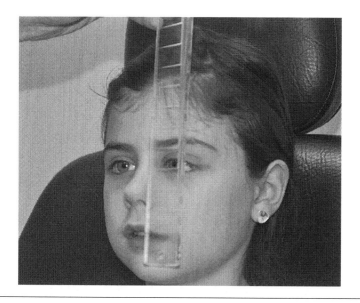

Free space prism bars being used to measure inward eye-teaming limits at near (target held just out of view to the left.) The doctor can watch the eyes to see when they stop teaming as well as listening to when the patient reports two (or blurred) images. The result gives the doctor a good indication of the strength of the converging system.

5. Vergence Facility Testing. This is arguably my favorite test because it provides a lot of information, in such a short time. It is highly correlated to reading and tracking ability. Using "base in and base-out prisms," it is a test that looks at how quickly you can move your eyes inwards and outwards, but this time in an *alternating sequence*. It tests the flexibility of the patient's oculomotor system. It can be done at a distance and at near. A typical result is about 15 cycles per minute at near and about 10 cycles per minute at a distance.

If someone fails this test, it tells you there is an inflexibility in the eye-teaming system; hence there will also very likely be difficulty controlling eye-teaming when reading.

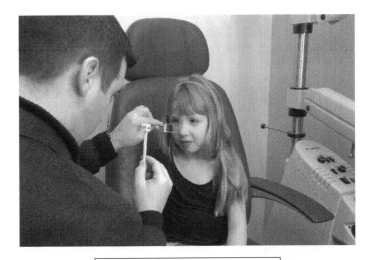

Near point vergence facility being tested

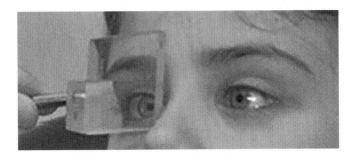

Close up view of vergence facility testing

6. Visagraph Testing / Infra-red Tracking Testing: In this test, the patient wears goggles that has four infra-red tracking cameras attached to it. It can track where the eyes are looking on the page, while the child reads, in real time. There is an image of the technology below.

This test not only measures the eye movements in real-time, but it also gives us valuable statistics. These metrics include the number of eye movements that are made when a patient reads 100 words. It counts subtle movements such as, how many times the eyes go backward on the line, how many times a line is skipped, in addition to the percentage of the time the eyes are looking at the same point, at the same time (Cross-Correlation) when reading.

This is an invaluable test and something that we published on, as it is an excellent objective assessment of reading mechanics, in terms of the physical eye movements being made when reading.

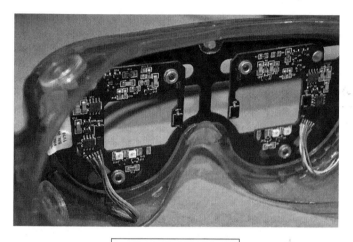

Image of visagraph system

Example of type of results given on testing

7. Fixation Disparity Testing: This testing looks at small, micro-misalignments of the eyes. The misalignment may after cause strain or headaches often and although not always, intermittent double vision at times.

The test involves the patient wearing a pair of red/green, or polarized glasses, and then looking at a "crosshair" type target, where one eye sees the red lines, and one eye sees the green lines (see below). The ideal scenario is that with the red/green or polarised glasses, the crosshairs look perfectly aligned. This means both eyes are looking at the same point in space on the X/Y axis, (the alignment on the vertical and horizontal lines). If the lines are misaligned either vertically or horizontally, then there is a "slip" in the alignment of the eyes, which needs to be corrected somehow, either with prisms, lenses or therapy-based interventions. If the lines (called Nonius lines) are aligned but unstable or moving, this tells the doctor that the eye alignment stability is not consistent.

Sometimes, we have seen patients get nauseous doing this test, similar to what happens when they watch a 3D movie. In order to see a 3D movie, you need a good eye alignment system that can move quickly enough to keep up with the motion on the screen. This is especially true of 3D movies on large screens in the movie theatre, as the larger area of motion often sets off symptoms, more than smaller screens. Concussion patients find this particularly problematic.

Testing of fixation disparity in a child

Picture of FD target and glasses used to test for
misalignment in clinic

Note that one eye sees two lines and one line sees "the other two" lines. Ideally, with both eyes open together, all four lines should be seen as stable and aligned. This test can also be done at distance (near test shown) using a polarized display.

8. Laser Pointer Test: This test is similar to the FD test above, but it has one difference. It gives results that make it very obvious to family members of patients if there is an issue or not. The set up is the same as above. The patient wears red/green glasses, however, and instead of using crosshairs; the patient holds a red laser pointer, while the doctor uses a green laser pointer.

The doctor shines the green laser pointer at a random point on the wall, and the patient points their red laser on top of the doctor's laser. If there is eye misalignment either vertically, horizontally or both (obliquely), then the patient will see the laser points as superimposed despite those watching and not wearing the glasses, seeing the red laser point and the green laser point as being in different places.

This is so useful, as light from a laser travels in a straight line, it can be used to assess eye alignment in a variety of eye positions and distances. Ideally, the results from this Laser Pointer Test should correlate with the Fixation Disparity testing. Diagnostically as a doctor, if I have two different tests that test the same function, and we set the same result, then the data is more reliable. It also prevents incorrect findings or false-positive results.

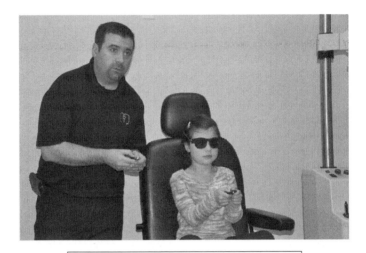

A child being tested for ocular misalignment in clinic

(The dots should be super-imposed. If not, it indicates an eye mis-alignment issue is present.)

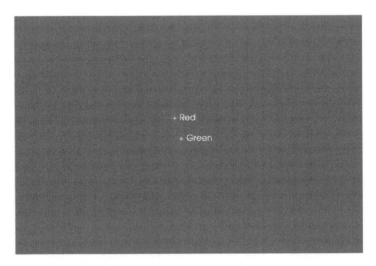

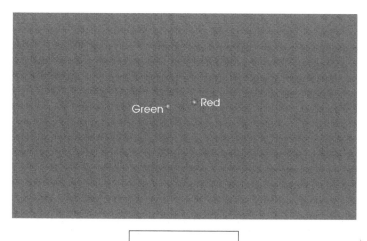

Small horizontal issue

Shown are examples of what parents would see despite the child saying, "Yes, they are aligned." Top shows a vertical misalignment and bottom shows horizontal misalignment. Sometimes a combination is found (i.e., oblique).

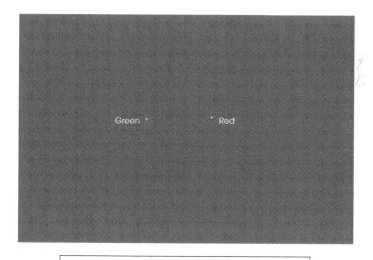

Larger horizontal issue

The patient, however, with the Red/Green glasses on will state that the dots are superimposed.

9. Hess Lancaster Test: This is a test that measures how well the eyes are aligned in different positions of gaze, at given set distances. If the eyes are perfectly aligned in every position, you will see an image like the one below, marked Normal. If the eyes are misaligned, there are dozens of patterns possible, and one example is shown in the image below, marked Abnormal. This test is not always required, but when odd patterns of eye alignment are difficult to diagnose, this test is helpful. The Hess Lancaster Test can be done on a computer, which is my preference, but can also be projected onto a wall, allowing the eyes to be tested at greater distances and to more extremes of eye positioning.

To see examples of the Hess charts go to http://zuhrick.com/hess/ to learn more.

10. Dynamic Retinoscopy: This is a test using a retinoscope (image below). A retinoscope shines a bright light of a particular pattern into the eye. The doctor then looks at the "reflex" reflecting back from the eye and interprets what is happening within the focusing mechanisms of the eye. This test can also be used in a routine eye exam to estimate a person's prescription for eyeglasses. Machines, called Autorefractors, however, have more or less taken over this role nowadays in routine eye exams.

The retinoscope, however, can be used for another invaluable purpose. The technique we often use is called Nott's Technique. In this test, the patient reads different types of text fonts off a card. They read naturally looking up close and with both eyes open. The doctor then uses the retinoscope to observe the focusing mechanism of the eyes while the patient reads.

If there is a significant "Lag Reflex" seen, it means that the eye is focusing further away than the card they are reading from, resulting in a strain on the system. If there is a "Lead Reflex" seen, however, then the eye is over-focussing, meaning the eye is trying to look at space in front of the card and still straining to do so.

This test also measures the brightness of the reflex observed. In other words, the brighter the reflex found, the more efficient the eye and the less it has to work. The doctor then observes the reflex of the eye, making the technique wholly objective, where the patient can say nothing subjective that could influence the result. Over the years, I have found dynamic retinoscopy to be invaluable. After all, the human eye is not a machine, but a living dynamic organism. Seeing its focusing ability in real time is an invaluable technique. Doctors need to dust off their retinoscopes more often.

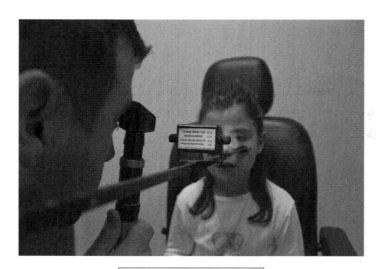

Dynamic retinoscopy in action

185

Retniscope with different focusing targets for
children of different ages

Hopefully, this chapter has given parents an overview of the 10 most commonly used tests we use to gather detailed information around eye-teaming or focussing issues during the VSA assessment. More tests can be done, but these are the most commonly used ones in our clinic. As Visual Memory, as shown in research done at Ohio State University, is a powerful predictor of reading level and mathematical ability, it is in essence, the "crowning jewel" of an intact oculomotor and visual processing system. It is the key visual skill that these oculomotor based visual skills exist to nourish. For without the fertile soil of intact visuals skills, the blooming flower of visual memory will never grow.

REFERENCES

Quaid Chapters

1. Felleman D.J., Van Essen D.C. (1991). Distributed Hierarchical Processing in the Primate Cerebral Cortex. *Cerebral Cortex*, 1(1); 1-47.

2. Quaid P.T., Simpson T.L. (2013). Association between Reading Speed, Cycloplegic Refractive Error and Oculomotor Function in Reading Disabled Children versus Controls. *Graefes Archives of Clinical & Experimental Ophthalmology*, 251; 169-187.

3. Learning Disabilities in Canada: Economic Costs to Individuals, Families and Society. *Roeher Institute Final Report and Executive Summary*, Jan 2002.

4. Major A., Maples W.C., Toomey S., DeRosier W., Gahn D. (2007). Variables Associated with the Incidence of Infantile Esotropia. Optometry, 78; 534-541.

5. Gesell A., Ilg F.L., Bullis G.E. (1950). Vision: Its Development in Infant and Child. *Hoeber Inc., Medical Book Department of Harper and Brothers*. New York, USA.

6. Manzo A.V., Manzo, U.C. (1995). Teaching Children to be Literate: A Reflective Approach. ISBN# 0-15-300560-2, Library of Congress Catalog Card # 93-80671.

7. Quaid P.T. (PhD thesis, 2005). Spatiotemporal Properties of Flicker Defined Form Illusory Contours (University of Waterloo School of Optometry & Vision Science, Ontario, Canada).

8. Mangen A., Walgermo B.R., Bronnick K. (2013). Reading

Linear Texts on Paper versus Computer Screen: Effects on Reading Comprehension. International Journal of Educational Research, 58; 61-68.

9. Kulp M.T., Edwards K.E., Mitchell B.S. (2002). Is Visual Memory Predictive of Below-Average Academic Achievement in Second through Fourth Graders? *Optometry & Vision Science*, 79(7); 431-434.

10. Kulp M.T., Earley M.J., Mitchell, G.L., Timmerman L.M., Frasco C.S., Geiger M.E. (2004). Are Visual Perceptual Skills Related to Mathematics Ability in Second through Sixth Grade Children? *Focus on Learning Problems in Mathematics*, 26(4); 44-51.

11. Lowel S., Singer W. (1992). Selection of Intrinsic Horizontal Connections in the Visual Cortex by Correlated Neuronal Activity. *Science*, 225, 209-212.

12. Raghuram A., Gowrisankaran S., Swanson E., Zurakowski D., Hunter D.G., Waber D.P. (2018). Frequency of Visual Deficits in Children with Developmental Dyslexia (along with DSM-V, Diagnostic & Statistical Manual, dyslexia section), *JAMA Ophthalmology*, Jul 2018, E1-E7.

13. Granet D.B., Gomi C.F., Ventura R., Miller-Scholte A. (2005). The Relationship between Convergence Insufficiency and ADHD. *Strabismus*, 13; 163-168.

14. Currie J., Stabile M., Jones L. (2014). Do Stimulant Medications Improve Educational and Behavioral Outcomes for Children with ADHD? *J. Health Economics*, 37; 58-69.

15. CITT Group (2008). A Randomized Clinical Trial of Treatments for Symptomatic Convergence Insufficiency in Children. *Archives of Ophthalmology*, 126(10); 1336-1349.

16. Borsting E. et al. (2012). Improvement in Academic Behaviours following Successful Treatment of Convergence Insufficiency. *Optometry & Vision Science*, 89(1); 12-18.

17. American Academy of Pediatrics (2011). ADHD: Clinical Practice Guidelines for the Diagnosis, Evaluation and

Treatment of Attention-Deficit / Hyperactivity Disorder in Children and Adolescents. *Pediatrics*, 128(5); 1007-1022.

18. Poltavski D.V., Biberdorf D., Petros T.V. (2012). Accommodative Response and Cortical Activity during Sustained Attention. *Vision Research*, 63; 1-8.

19. Book: Ocular Anatomy & Histology (Pipe & Rapley). The Gresham Press, Surrey, UK.

20. Vaughn W., Maples W.C., Hoenes R. (2006). The Association between Vision QoL and Academics as Measured by the College of Optometrists in Vision Development QoL Questionnaire. *Optometry*, 77; 116-123.

21. Quaid P.T., Cunningham D.J. (2019). Effect of Optometric Vision Therapy on a Cohort of Children with Reading based Learning Difficulties. *Presented at the COVD Annual Conference, 2019 (49th Annual Conference, Kansas, USA).*

22. https://www.readingrockets.org/article/it-reading-disorder-or-developmental-lag

23. https://dyslexiaida.org/universal-screening-k-2-reading/

24. https://www.ncbi.nlm.nih.gov/pmc/articles/PMC5393968/pdf/nihms793373.pdf

Beginning to See

1. Major A, Maples WC, Toomey S, DeRosier W, Gahn D. Variables associated with the incidence of infantile esotropia. Optometry 2007;78:534-541.

The Miracle of Vision

1. Johnson, S.P., Development of the Visual System in Neural Circuit Development and Function in the Brain, 2013

2. Gesell, A, Vision: Its Development in Infant and Child; Hoeber 1949

3. Gesell, A. and Amatruda, C.S., Developmental Diagnosis; chapter 13 Blindness; Hoeber 1941

4. Gesell, A. Infant Vision; Scientific American February 1950

5. Meltzoff and Brooks, The Development of Gaze following and its relation to language, Developmental Science 8:6 (2005) pp 535-543

6. Steele, G.T., The Circle of Understanding first described 2018

Collaboration & Coordination

1. Musel, B., et al., Retinotopic and lateralized processing of spatial frequencies in human visual cortex during scene categorization. J Cogn Neurosci, 2013. 25(8): p. 1315-31.

2. Parraga, C.A., T. Troscianko, and D.J. Tolhurst, The human visual system is optimised for processing the spatial information in natural visual images. Curr Biol, 2000. 10(1): p. 35-8.

3. Zetterberg, C., H.O. Richter, and M. Forsman, Temporal Co-Variation between Eye Lens Accommodation and Trapezius Muscle Activity during a Dynamic Near-Far Visual Task. PLoS One, 2015. 10(5): p. e0126578.

4. Ehlers, J., et al., Pupil Size Changes as an Active Information Channel for Biofeedback Applications. Appl Psychophysiol Biofeedback, 2016. 41(3): p. 331-9.

5. Reimer, J., et al., Pupil fluctuations track rapid changes in adrenergic and cholinergic activity in cortex. Nat Commun, 2016. 7: p. 13289.

6. Ciulla, M.M., et al., Vascular network changes in the retina during ageing in normal subjects: a computerized quantitative analysis. Ital Heart J, 2000. 1(5): p. 361-4.

7. Tavares Ferreira, J., et al., Retina and Choroid of Diabetic Patients without observed retinal vascular changes: a Longitudinal Study. Am J Ophthalmol, 2017.

8. Chatterjee, P.R., et al., Estimation of tear glucose level and its role as a prompt indicator of blood sugar level. J Indian Med Assoc, 2003. 101(8): p. 481-3.

9. Chu, M.X., et al., Soft contact lens biosensor for in situ monitoring of tear glucose as non-invasive blood sugar assessment. Talanta, 2011. 83(3): p. 960-5.

10. Leung, T.S., et al., Screening neonatal jaundice based on the sclera color of the eye using digital photography. Biomed Opt Express, 2015. 6(11): p. 4529-38.

11. Ozge, G., et al., Retina nerve fiber layer and choroidal thickness changes in obstructive sleep apnea syndrome. Postgrad Med, 2016. 128(3): p. 317-22.

12. Kessel, L., et al., Sleep disturbances are related to decreased transmission of blue light to the retina caused by lens yellowing. Sleep, 2011. 34(9): p. 1215-9.

13. Richter, H.O., T. Banziger, and M. Forsman, Eye-lens accommodation load and static trapezius muscle activity. Eur J Appl Physiol, 2011. 111(1): p. 29-36.

14. Miralles, R., et al., Visual input effect on EMG activity of sternocleidomastoid and masseter muscles in healthy subjects and in patients with myogenic cranio-cervical-mandibular dysfunction. Cranio, 1998. 16(3): p. 168-84.

15. Mavritsaki, E., et al., Bridging the gap between physiology and behavior: evidence from the sSoTS model of human visual attention. Psychol Rev, 2011. 118(1): p. 3-41.

16. Roberg, B.L., et al., Speedy eye movements in multiple sclerosis: association with performance on visual and nonvisual cognitive tests. J Clin Exp Neuropsychol, 2015. 37(1): p. 1-15.

17. Sinclair, J.R., A.L. Jacobs, and S. Nirenberg, Selective ablation of a class of amacrine cells alters spatial processing in the retina. J Neurosci, 2004. 24(6): p. 1459-67.

18. Grutersa, K., Murphy, D., Groh, J., et al. The eardrums move when the eyes move: A multisensory effect on the mechanics

of hearing. Proceedings of the National Academy of Sciences PNAS, 2018. 115(6):201717948 DOI: 10.1073/pnas.1717948115 www.pnas.org/cgi/doi/10.1073/pnas.1717948115

Understanding the IEP

1. Ontario Ministry of Education. The Individual Education Plan (IEP): A Resource Guide. Toronto: Queen's Printer for Ontario, 2004. http://www.edu.gov.on.ca/eng/general/elemsec/speced/guide/resource/iepresguid.pdf
2. Ontario Ministry of Education. *The Individual Education Plan (IEP): A Resource Guide, 2004.* (Toronto: Queen's Printer for Ontario, 2004), http://www.edu.gov.on.ca/eng/general/elemsec/speced/guide/resource/iepresguid.pdf

Seeing in Three Dimensions

1. Barry, SR. Fixing My Gaze: A Scientist's Journey into Seeing in Three Dimensions. New York: Basic Books, 2009.
2. Borsting E and the CITT study group. 2012. Improvement in academic behaviors after successful treatment of convergence insufficiency.
3. Optometry and Vision Science 89: 12-18.
4. Convergence Insufficiency Treatment Trial Study Group. 2008.
5. Randomized clinical trial of treatments for symptomatic convergence insufficiency in children. Archives of Ophthalmology 126: 1336-49.
6. Kanonidou E, Proudlock FA, and Gottlob I. 2010. Reading strategies in mild to moderate strabismic amblyopia: An eye movement investigation.
7. Investigative Ophthalmology and Visual Science 51: 3502-08.
8. Levi D. M., Song S., Pelli D. (2007). Amblyopic reading is

crowded.

9. Journal of Vision 7, article 21, 1–17.

10. Lions C, Bui-Quoc E, Seassau M, Bucci MP. 2013. Binocular coordination of saccades during reading in strabismic children.

11. Investigative Ophthalmology and Visual Science 54: 620-28.

VUE³
Vision Therapy

The VUE³ Vision Therapy Clinics
www.vuetherapy.ca

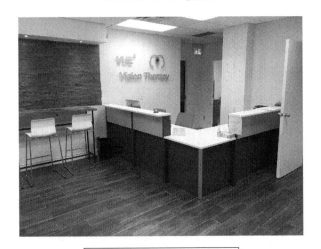

Guelph Vision Therapy Center

105-195 Hanlon Creek Boulevard
Guelph, ON Canada N1C 0A1
Phone: 519-265-8895
E-mail: info@vuetherapy.ca

Toronto Clinic

North York Vision Therapy Center
404-491 Lawrence Avenue West
North York, ON Canada M5M 1C7
Phone: 416-855-1686
Fax: 416-630-9655
E-mail: northyork@vuetherapy.ca

"Our clinic name is pronounced "View Cubed" to reflect Canada being bilingual (Vue = seen) and the fact that we work to restore three dimensional vision. The E can also be "cubed" as we stand for "Empowering the child, Embracing change and Enhancing vision".

RESOURCES

www.covd.org

Here are some other helpful resources recommended by Dr. Quaid.

New Hope for Concussions TBI & PTSD by Dr. Lawrence D Komer, Joan Chandler Komer and contributors Dr. William S. Cook Jr., Dr. G. Blair Lamb, Andrew Marr, Dr. Patrick T. Quaid. (Peak Performance Institute Inc.)

Fixing My Gaze: A Scientist's Journey Into Seeing in Three Dimensions (Basic Books)

The Ghost in My Brain: How a Concussion Stole My Life and How the New Science of Brain Plasticity Helped Me Get It Back by Dr. Clair Elliot (Penguin Books)

Jillian's Story: How Vision Therapy Changed My Daughter's Life by Jillian Benoit and Robin Benoit (The Small Press)

Thinking Goes to School: Piaget's Theory in Practice by Hans G. Furth and Harry Wachs (Oxford University Press)

See It. Say It. Do It! The Parent's & Teacher's Action Guide to Creating Successful Students & Confident Kids by Dr. Lynn F. Hellerstein (HiClear Publishing LLC)

Vision and Learning: How Undiagnosed Vision Problems Cause Learning Difficulties and What You Can Do to Unlock Your Child's Academic Potential - A Guide for Parents and Professionals by Heike Schuhmacher M.D. (CreateSpace)

In the classic book entitled, "Teaching Your Child to be Literate: A Reflective Approach," written by two prominent experts in the learning process field, (Anthony Manzo is a cognitive psychologist & Ula Manzo is a professor emeritus from California State University at Fullerton. Some fascinating statements are made very much in line with the thoughts laid out in this chapter.

In particular, chapter 5 on reading and responding and chapter 6 on word recognition and analysis are very much in line with the notion of the importance of visual memory. The term "selective attention" can be found in the book too. This wonderful term perfectly describes the notion that a child has to look at a word, and remember how it is spelled – even though it looks different than how it sounds.

This ability falls apart when visual memory skills are deficient. This would result in a persistently phonetic pattern of spelling. This pattern is seen in our clinic in dyseidetic cases all the time!

CONTRIBUTORS

Susan R. Barry, Ph.D.

(Photo of Dr. Barry by Rosalie Winard)

Susan R. Barry is Professor Emeritus of Biological Sciences and Professor Emeritus of Neuroscience and Behavior at Mount Holyoke College. She earned her B.A. in biology from Wesleyan University in 1976 and Ph.D. in biology from Princeton University in 1981. For years, she taught her neurobiology students the conventional, scientific wisdom that stereovision could develop only during a critical period in early childhood. She even used her own vision history to support this dogma since she had been cross-eyed since early infancy and was stereoblind. However, at age forty-eight, she consulted developmental optometrist, Dr. Theresa Ruggiero, who prescribed a program of optometric vision therapy. To her utter astonishment, her vision improved dramatically. She could read and drive for longer periods without tiring, and she experienced her first 3D views. Dubbed "Stereo

Sue" by Oliver Sacks in a 2006 New Yorker article by that name, Dr. Barry has gone on to write her own book *Fixing My Gaze: A Scientist's Journey into Seeing in Three Dimensions* (Basic Books, 2009) which was rated the fourth best science book for 2009 by the editors of Amazon.com, selected as one of the best sci-tech books of 2009 by the Library Journal, and has been translated into six languages.

Stephanie Beaudette

Stephanie was born in Atlantic Canada and due to her father's military career ended up in Ottawa, Ontario. Stephanie completed a two year Law Clerk program at Algonquin College and worked as a Legal Assistant for four years prior to deciding to go back to University. She was accepted to the Applied Human Nutrition program at the University of Guelph and moved from Ottawa in 2012.

After graduation, Stephanie took a full-time job with Dr. Quaid as the Office Manager of VUE[3] Vision Therapy and has since moved to the role of Chief Operations Officer.

Stephanie met her husband in 2009, and they have one child together.

Toni Bristol

Toni Bristol is President and Founder of Expansion Consultants, Inc. which is located in Los Angeles, California. Toni began consulting health care practices in 1984 and started specializing in vision therapy practice management, public relations and marketing in 1988. For more than 30 years, she has helped thousands of optometrists in the U.S., Canada, Australia, and Malaysia.

For approximately 10 years, Toni was the Public Relations consultant for the College of Optometrists in Vision Development (COVD) and assisted in starting the "Making Vision Therapy Visible" campaign, while maintaining her consulting practice.

Toni has served COVD for more than 13 years as a member of the President's Advisory Council. She has received the prestigious COVD President's Award three times for her many contributions, 2003, 2008 and 2015.

Born and raised in New York City, her father, a dentist and associate professor at Columbia University, instilled Toni, with his passion for public health.

As an adult, Toni went through a vision therapy program, and her granddaughter is also going through vision therapy.

Dr. Daniel J. Cunningham, O.D., FCOVD

Born in Northern Ontario, Dr. Cunningham always had a spirit of adventure. After completing his undergraduate studies at the University of Waterloo, he moved to Texas where he married his wife, Jennifer. Dr. Cunningham graduated from Nova Southeastern University's College of Optometry in 2004 in Fort Lauderdale, Florida and went on to become board certified in the USA in vision development, vision therapy, and vision rehabilitation.

After graduation, Dr. Cunningham joined a private practice in Bethesda, Maryland where he honed his vision therapy skills. He would go on to practice optometric vision therapy in Annapolis, Maryland, and Windsor, Ontario before joining Dr. Patrick Quaid at VUE[3] Vision Therapy in Guelph and North York, Ontario.

Dr. Cunningham has had the honor of lecturing on the topic of optometric vision therapy to optometrists, therapists, parents, and allied health care professionals over the course of his career. Dr. Cunningham has contributed to the vast research database on optometric vision therapy with his time spent as Chief of Clinic Services for VUE[3] Vision Therapy.

In 2019 Dr. Cunningham will celebrate his 20th wedding anniversary with his wife, Jennifer. Together they are raising their vibrant 3-year-old daughter, Imogen.

Karen M. Fairley

Karen "Cari" Fairley is an elementary school educator with more than 25 years experience in three boards of education in Ontario, Canada. For 12 years, she taught junior and senior kindergarten with what is now the Toronto Board of Education. She was a Grade 2 teacher at the Peel Region Board of Education. In the Greater Essex Country District School Board, she taught primary vocal music, Grade 2, primary and junior art, and Grade 5. Her new assignment is a Grade 2 elementary class.

She is an advocate of teaching through the arts. In 2005, she was featured on a DVD called, "Bringing Curriculum to Life." Her classrooms always feature large displays to encourage creativity and engagement in her students. "True Treasure," a picture book that she created with her Grade 2 class, was published by her Director of Education. Each of the students received a copy. Copies were also given to administration and trustees in her board. The Provincial Minister of Education and the Premier of Ontario were also presented with a copy of the collaborative book.

In 2018, Cari received an honor from the Mayor of Windsor, and was awarded the first, "Community Champion Award." The award recognized her contributions to her community through her teaching and for a nutrition partnership she fostered with local churches. Her inner-city school has for the past ten years, benefited from an additional snack of fresh fruits and vegetables.

Cari enjoys being an Associate Teacher, with student teachers from the Faculties of Education from the University of Toronto, Queen's University, York University, the University of Western Ontario, Brock University, and the University of Windsor. She is also a senior teacher mentoring new teachers.

In addition to teaching, Cari is a corporate seminar speaker, enjoys painting on natural elements such as rocks and driftwood, and is a church soloist.

She, and her husband, Grant, live in Ontario, Canada.

Jenny Fountain

Jenny Fountain is a Vice-Principal with the Greater Essex County District School Board. She has 25 years of teaching experience in the elementary panel. More than half of her teaching career has been spent working with inner-city youth and Syrian refugees. Over the past 20 years, she has served as an associate teacher for aspiring teacher candidates and ECE students. Currently, she is serving as the Ontario Principal's Council representative on the GECDSB Mental Health Steering Committee.

She earned a Master of Education degree in Curriculum Studies from the University of Windsor and has a specialist certificate in Special Education from Queen's University.

Jenny lives with her husband, Ken and their three children, Cody, Jessica and Aidan, in Ontario, Canada. Jenny and Ken are active in their local church and support three foster children through Compassion Canada. In her spare time, she and her husband volunteer at a local animal rescue and have spent the last several years fostering abandoned kittens and rehoming rehabilitated feral cats.

WC Maples, O.D., FCOVD

Dr. Maples received his B.S. in geography and chemistry from the University of Southern Mississippi (USM) in 1964 and his Doctor of Optometry from Southern College of Optometry (SCO) in 1968. His Master of Science in Community Health Education was earned in 1977 from USM.

He began a general practice of optometry in Wiggins, Mississippi from 1968 to 1980. He also began a specialty practice in vision development and vision rehabilitation in Gulfport, Mississippi where he practiced from 1972. After building these two practices, he subsequently sold both practices in 1980 to accept a position at Northeastern State University: Oklahoma College of Optometry (NSU-OCO) in 1981. He designed the vision therapy clinic and protocol for the college clinic that was housed in the WW Hastings Indian Hospital in Tahlequah, Oklahoma. He served as the chief of clinic for 15 years. He retired from NSU-OCO in 2006 as a professor emeritus. He later accepted a clinical professorship at his alma mater (SCO) and served there for five years before retiring to Hattiesburg, Mississippi in 2011. Dr. Maples remains active in the profession by lecturing both domestically and internationally. In 2016 he again entered private practice in Hattiesburg, Mississippi (Bellevue Specialty Eye Clinic) where he continues to see patients.

Dr. Maples is a Fellow of the American Academy of Optometry (AAO); a Fellow of the Australasian College of Behavioral Optometry (ACBO) and a Fellow of the College of Optometrists in Vision Development (COVD). He earned his FCOVD in 1972 and is the oldest active fellow member of this board certifying organization.

Dr. Maples has served on the Board of COVD with two years as president of this organization. He has served on the International Examination and Certification Board (IECB) of COVD on several occasions with three years as the Chair of the IECB.

He has always been active in research as well as clinic and is well-published in many peer-reviewed journals both domestically and internationally. He was awarded a lifetime achievement award from SCO in 2011. In addition, he serves his community. He was president of the Tahlequah Kiwanis club and a member for 24 years. He was voted Citizen of the Year for this city. As a Marine, he has been active in the United States Marine Corps League for 20 years. He has also been active in his churches, being a Sunday School teacher for 30+ years.

He has lectured and does lecture domestically and internationally on every continent except Antarctica.

Privately, he is married with three adult children, eight grandchildren and 3 great-grandchildren. He enjoys travel, sailing (as a deckhand) and gardening.

Glen Steele, O.D., FCOVD

Dr. Glen Steele, a Professor of Pediatric Optometry at the Southern College of Optometry in Memphis, places a special emphasis on the vision care needs of the infant and child. Following graduation from Southern College of Optometry, he completed a fellowship at the prestigious Gesell Institute of Child Development. Glen is the past president of both the College of Optometrists in Vision Development and the Optometric Extension Program Foundation and past chair of the American Optometric Association InfantSEE® Committee. He is also a member of the Continuing Education Committee for SECO International. Dr. Steele holds fellowship in the College of Optometrists in Vision Development and the American Academy of Optometry and has been inducted into the National Academies of Practice.

He has served the AOA, SECO International, COVD and the OEPF in many capacities. He has lectured extensively throughout the U.S. and internationally in the area of vision development and care in the infant and young child. He has presented oral and poster presentations at a number of multi-disciplinary meetings.

Dr. Steele has been selected as Tennessee's Optometrist of the Year, one of Optometric Management's Top Ten Optometrists of the Decade, and the G.N. Getman Award from the College of Optometrists in Vision Development. He was awarded Southern College of Optometry's Lifetime Achievement Award in 2001. He has been a Behavioral Scholar in Residence at the New England College of Optometry. Dr. Steele also received Prevent Blindness Tennessee's Lifetime of Service Award, the John Streff award from Neuro-Optometric Rehabilitation Association, and the Armand Bastien Award for International Accomplishments in 2010 and the Skeffington Alexander Award in 2014 from the International Congress of Behavioral Optometry. In 2011, he was awarded the William Feinbloom Award from the American Academy of Optometry. He has been presented the Visionary Award by the Tennessee Public Health Association and the Distinguished Service Award from the American Public Health Association Vision Care Section in 2018. At the 2019 Optometry's Meeting (AOA), Glen was inducted into the National Optometry Hall of Fame.

The Fors/Steele Developmental Vision Endowed Scholarship has been established jointly in his name along with the late L. Allen Fors, O.D. at the Southern College of Optometry.

Dr. Deborah Zelinsky, O.D., FCOVD

Deborah Zelinsky, O.D. is an optometrist noted worldwide for her work in neuro-optometric rehabilitation. Currently, she serves as founder and executive research director of the Mind-Eye Institute, based in Northbrook, Illinois.

The Institute provides a platform for her to continue studies of how changes in ambient lighting affect brain function, which impacts a person's spatial awareness, movement, and selective attention to sound.

Her global reputation is due, in part, to her development of the Z-Bell TestSM, a revolutionary method of evaluating a patient's overall spatial processing and ability to integrate retinal signals with the perception of auditory space. The test allows Dr. Zelinsky and her team to prescribe lenses and other optometric interventions that normalize the balance between central and peripheral receptors in the retina while enhancing the interaction between eyes and ears.

Studies show that autistic children do not synchronize eyes and ears, and in the second edition of "Outsmarting Autism," Patricia Lemer mentions the Z-BellSM testing.

In addition to her work with the Mind-Eye Institute, Dr. Zelinsky is a fellow in both the College of Optometrists in Vision Development and the Neuro-Optometric Rehabilitation Association, a board member of the Society for Brain Mapping and a community leader for the Society of Neuroscience.

ABOUT THE AUTHOR

Dr. Patrick T. Quaid (Optometrist, MCOptom, FCOVD, Ph.D.) is a practitioner, researcher, author, and lecturer on vision development. Dr. Quaid mainly deals with the treatment of visual dysfunction both in concussion-related cases and learning difficulty related cases.

He is an Adjunct Professor (University of Waterloo School of Optometry & Vision Science, Ontario, Canada) and CEO of VUE³ Vision Therapy Clinics (www.vuetherapy.ca) in addition to currently serving on the Board of Directors for COVD International (College of Optometrists in Vision Development, www.covd.org, USA based not-for-profit group).

Originally from the Republic of Ireland, Dr. Quaid studied Statistical Mathematics and subsequently trained as an Optometrist in the U.K. (University of Bradford School of Optometry) and subsequently worked in the U.K. Hospital Eyecare System (Moorfield's Eye Hospital, London & Bradford Royal Infirmary, West Yorkshire.)

Dr. Quaid was awarded his Ph.D. in Vision Science at the University of Waterloo School of Optometry & Vision Science in 2005 in addition to completing a Post-Doctorate funded by the Canadian Institute of Health Research (CIHR). Dr. Quaid's Ph.D. thesis and postdoctoral research aided in the development of an early detection device for glaucoma (Heidelberg Edge Perimeter) which is now in commercial use.

He has published several papers as first author in high impact optometry and ophthalmology journals such as Investigative Ophthalmology and Vision Science and Graefe's Archives of Clinical & Experimental Ophthalmology on topics related to both glaucoma and the challenging area of binocular vision dysfunction and how it relates to learning disabilities and concussion based injuries.

Dr. Quaid frequently lends his expertise as a speaker and a writer on a variety of topics related to vision health. He has spoken at venues such as Ohio State, Berkeley, McMaster University Medical School, University of Western Ontario Medical School in addition to concussion-based lectures for the University Health Network (UHN) in Toronto. Dr. Quaid has also given interviews to numerous media outlets (including CBC) across Canada on the topic of Binocular Vision dysfunction and its relationship to 3-D Technology.

In addition to his Ph.D. and Postdoctoral training, Dr. Quaid has also completed a Fellowship with the College of Optometrists & Vision Development (USA Board Certification designation in the area of Rehabilitative Vision Therapy). In 2013, Dr. Quaid was recognized by the COVD for his research, (Best Research paper on a novel 3-step test for predicting Hess patterns from eye movements in the clinic.)

Dr. Quaid has also in the past provided consulting services to Heidelberg, (Germany), Carl Zeiss Meditec (USA) and Nikon Canada (Montreal) on topics from glaucoma to eye movement disorder.

In January 2014, Dr. Quaid opened the Guelph Vision Therapy Centre (now called " VUE³" Clinics pronounced, "view-cubed"), which was the first clinic in Canada of its kind to integrate clinical management and research into a "clinical translational research" model which allows data to be tracked on all treated patients to validate the effectiveness of optometric vision therapy. Dr. Quaid very much supports collaborative care models in an effort to deal with the ramifications of visual dysfunction both in the concussion domain and in the visually related learning difficulties domain. Dr. Quaid's clinic has also received support from the Canadian Government (SR&ED grants) to conduct research in his clinics into better means of detection and management of visually related problems in concussion cases and learning difficulty cases.

Dr. Quaid regularly lectures at the University of Waterloo School of Optometry program and also at the University of Guelph (Kinesiology program) on the topic of eye movement disorders.

In 2019, Dr. Quaid was given the NORA award in recognition of his work for the "Advancement of Neuro-Optometric Rehabilitation." At the same ceremony, Dr. Eric Singman, MD PhD (Chief of Neuro-Ophthamology at Johns Hopkins University) received this prestigious, multidisciplinary award for co-authoring a landmark chapter on visual dysfunction in concussion with Dr. Quaid. The Neuro-Optometric Rehabilitation Association (NORA) is based in the United States and is focused on visual issues related to brain injury.

Privately, Dr. Quaid is happily married to his wife of 15 years, has two children, and loves to write calligraphy in his spare time - ideally, while also listening to Frank Sinatra!

Zuhrick Publishing
a division of Zuhrick Inc.
www.zuhrick.com

Manufactured by Amazon.ca
Bolton, ON

10435105R00127